Without Warning & Only Sometimes

Also by Kit de Waal

Fiction

My Name is Leon

The Trick to Time

Supporting Cast

Six Foot Six

Becoming Dinah

As Editor

Common People

Without Warning & Only Sometimes

Scenes from an Unpredictable Childhood

KIT DE WAAL

TINDER
PRESS

First published in Great Britain in 2022 by Tinder Press
An imprint of HEADLINE PUBLISHING GROUP

1

Cataloguing in Publication Data is available from the British Library

Hardback ISBN 978 1 4722 8483 9
Trade paperback ISBN 978 1 4722 8484 6

Designed and typeset by CM&EN
Printed and bound in Great Britain by Clays Ltd, Elcograf S.p.A.

Headline's policy is to use papers that are natural, renewable and recyclable
products and made from wood grown in well-managed forests and other
controlled sources. The logging and manufacturing processes are expected
to conform to the environmental regulations of the country of origin.

HEADLINE PUBLISHING GROUP
An Hachette UK Company
Carmelite House
50 Victoria Embankment
London EC4Y 0DZ

www.tinderpress.co.uk
www.headline.co.uk
www.hachette.co.uk

For

Sheila Doyle and Arthur O'Loughlin,

with love

'We never shall have any more time. We have, and we have always had, all the time there is'

Arnold Bennett, *How to Live on 24 Hours a Day*

Contents

1

I Will Die

I will die.

I will die for wanting Christmas, for the slip of red ribbon from a huge box, for dreaming of the presents inside, Fry's Chocolate Cream, things off the telly, other children's presents. I will die for a taste of turkey and the imagined feel of the frilly white cuffs around its juicy brown leg. I will die for the dream of a mince pie I have never tasted and the magic blue flame on a Christmas pudding. Just the picture of it. I will die because I want to pull a cracker, because I want to wear a hat. I didn't know about the jokes inside, I didn't know about the little gift. I will find out about them when I am seventeen.

I will die because I want a birthday party.

I will die for my grinding embarrassment when the teacher halts the school assembly before the worship bit starts so that me and my sister can walk out. And I will die for the shame I feel when I walk back in again past superior girls and sniggering boys in time for the announcement of detentions and who won the Art Prize, who won the English Prize. My sister, usually.

I will die because while I sit outside assembly and they sing 'There is a Green Hill Far Away', I sing along but only in my heart. Worst of all, in my heart.

I will die when the earthquakes start. I will be walking to school and the pavement will rumble and hiccup and a crack will start under my feet, small at first, and nobody else will realize what's happening, but I will know that the end has come. Then the road splits in a zigzag fracture and the tarmac breaks in half and the buses tip in and the cars and lamp posts, and if there are any women with prams, they'll tumble in too, and dogs and motorbikes and trees and shops and anyone walking home with bread or potatoes, in they'll go. Everyone who doesn't believe. Or anyone who does believe but doesn't do as they should. In they'll go, toppling sideways into the chasm with their mouths open, screaming for forgiveness, but it's too late because they had their chance, we all had our chance. And when we are dead, the earth will close over us so the world can heal.

I skip the cracked paving stones on my way to school because it can start at any time, the Wrath of God, any moment, without warning. 'Stay on the watch! You do not know the day or the hour.' Kim doesn't know and Tracey doesn't know, nor Dean, nor Karen. Not even Mom. So I stay alert, ready to straddle the split if it's not too wide or outrun it by dashing around the corner or in the opposite direction or maybe straight inside someone's house, begging them to save me.

But even if I escape the earthquakes, there are so many other ways to die. The tower blocks will collapse, the lightning will strike or the angels themselves, disguised as ordinary men like when they came for Lot, like when they appeared to Abraham. They will call round to 70 Springfield Road, Moseley, Birmingham, looking for me, for me in particular, me by name. I will not be forgotten when the end comes.

Three times every week I am reminded that the world will end and I will die. We put on thin coats, my brother, my sisters and I, thin coats and not-good shoes, and if it's raining, we won't have an umbrella, and if it's snowing, that's just too bad. We squelch our way down to the bus stop, we shudder on plastic seats, we get off the bus early because it's cheaper than letting it take us all the way there.

Only Kim wants to go and worship. She's older than me and seems to understand better than the rest of us. She has let it into her heart and it has made her good. She talks about the Word of God all the way there and puts my mother straight on the original Greek, on the disciples' intent. We each have a Bible and our *Awake!* or

Watchtower magazine. We have fat books of explanation, we have a songbook each with a pink leather cover, we have pamphlets and papers, pens to underline the answers, pencils and a rubber in case we are wrong. We carry it all in cold, reluctant hands, all the way there, shamed if we see children we know, going somewhere exciting that doesn't involve God and Jesus and imminent death.

We're never early, never late. The Kingdom Hall of Jehovah's Witnesses, an old building halfway up a narrow road in a shabby part of south Birmingham, is cold and damp, hard seats, paraffin heaters, crackling lights. We sit in rows of six, but not near the front because that's where the Greeks sit week in and week out on invisible reservations, in their beige skin and slick suits, in posh dresses and gold clips in their thick black hair. It begins with a song.

Jehovah made a promise because he loves us so
To cleanse the earth of evil, of pain, of sin, of woe
He'll usher in a pure clean world for all of us who sigh
A Paradise, a Paradise, where we will never die!

Our mother croons and raises her chin to the Lord. This is the highlight of her week. We know the stories of her years in London in stockings and tight skirts, traipsing around town to see Ella Fitzgerald, singing along with Billy Eckstine, 'so handsome, so handsome', worshipping Nat King Cole and his velvet tongue, 'Let There Be Love'. We know she was a waitress in a coffee bar in Irish Kilburn, that she spent her money on records and concerts before she met our father. She gathers up her memories and pours them into Kingdom Melody number 106, throws her head back and closes her eyes and lingers on the last note. Too loud, too long. Someone turns round and looks. I crumple inside.

Two hours on a Thursday, two hours on a Sunday, we repeat the trip to the Kingdom Hall, and then every Tuesday there's one dreaded and intimate hour of House Meeting in the cramped, airless front room of a faithful family, the seats arranged in crushed rows, a Bible on each lap with nowhere to hide and a silence that crawls on the skin. At least the Thursday and Sunday meetings allow for some whispering and giggling. Only laughter and derision get us through it.

Me and Tracey and Dean give each Brother and Sister a name. Brother Westhouse has big ears and when we sit behind him his head looks like a trophy. So we call him 'First Place'. Sister Liddiard, who nods constantly with Parkinson's, is 'Yes, Miss'. Two brothers who take their ministry so seriously that they never smile are 'Holy' and 'Most Holy'. No one escapes. These are the crimes I will die for.

Time does not pass. The clock does not move. We each sit in our own miserable world of wishing it would end, hoping the speaker makes a mistake, maybe someone trips on their way to the stage, maybe a baby will cry, someone will make a faux pas in their talk, lose their place in the scriptures, fluff their lines. Maybe I can go to the toilet and take ages to wash my hands and then loiter at the back and not be made to return to my seat by 'Evil Eye' Edgar, who patrols the vestibule in his zoot suit and shuffle shoes. Maybe when it's all over, Brother Herbert, who has no nickname because he loves us and we love him, will say 'Come,' and extract from the bottomless pocket of his pin-stripe suit a boiled sweet, and this tall black man, dapper as my father, will smile and say something nice, something human that lets me feel good and not bad.

But there are ages yet to wait. I sit and fidget and cough and turn the pages of the Bible to and fro, to and fro, until there is nothing left to do and I am stretched to the edge of my patience, beyond the limits of my childhood goodness. I am missing *Top of the Pops*. I am missing *Monty Python*. I won't know what to say at school when everyone else talks about the dead parrot. What's so funny about a dead parrot? I will have to pretend.

Then there is the final song and prayer. I live with the dread that one day when my young muscles rebel, can take no more stillness and the brutal confinement of my very self, I will stand and strip naked and burst out of my skin. Not today, please not today. My breath becomes shallow. I tuck both hands under my thighs. I tuck it all inside, the guilt and shame, the longing and fear, all of it tucked under the twenty-ton hush of the Kingdom Hall and Jehovah's omniscient eye.

I won't burst out of my skin until I am twenty-one.

2

Black Nana

Black Nana's favourite place is sitting on a rocking chair in the middle room downstairs where the French windows lead out to a narrow passage between the house and the fence.

She's been there forever, sitting all day with Tracey on her long lap. She lets the baby play with her beads, lets her nibble Ritz Crackers with her fat little fingers and bounces her gently up and down. She talks to her in the slow, deep voice she keeps just for Tracey and Dad, thick with honey and foreign words. She has another voice for me and Kim and Mom, English. Sharp. Short. Clipped.

We wait until Black Nana's engrossed in her love, whispering and kissing and tickling, then me and Kim sneak out of the French windows and play quietly together in the garden as far away from her as we can get.

But if it's raining, we're stuck inside listening to the creak of the rocking chair, the coo-cooing of Black Nana smothering the big-eyed Tracey with love and treats. I watch. Kim watches.

Mom goes to work really early so Black Nana has to get us up for school in the morning. She makes us get dressed in our school uniform, a green skirt and a green jumper with a V-neck and red stripe that Mom has knitted for us and a white shirt with a green-and-red tie in a Windsor knot. Dad says no other knot will do. Because it's my first day, Mom took me to Start-Rite to buy new shoes and we both had our feet measured with a special machine. Both the same, me and Kim.

Black Nana carries Tracey downstairs even though she's nearly three, and me and Kim have to follow her all the way down and around the crook where the wide steps need two feet and into the back room by the kitchen. The mornings are dark and cold without Mom to light the fire and we are silent as we sit and wait for our porridge. The steamed-up windows weep into grey pools on the sill.

I don't know where Tracey goes while Black Nana makes the porridge, but it's just me and Kim at the table, our legs not swinging on the wooden chairs. Maybe Tracey sits on our grandmother's hip listening to her sing songs from back home, the ones that wither on her lips when Mom returns from work. Maybe Tracey's playing on the floor under our feet or lying down with a biscuit.

Before she puts the porridge on the table, Black Nana's long teak fingers fashion a sort of bowl out of waxed bread paper with MOTHER'S PRIDE written in red and white on the side. She presses the edges around and around until it forms itself into a shallow dish that she places in front of our silence.

Then she puts a dish of porridge on the table for each of us and we watch with desperate eyes as she sprinkles a meagre pinch of sugar on the dry, leathery skin. Kim portions the sugar out, a few grains for each spoonful to make the medicine go down, but I scoop all the sugar off in one go and eat it in one beautiful, sweet moment of joy. Then comes the misery of finishing it all up, fishing out the gluey lumps and dropping them into the paper bowl in front of us, one by one.

'Hurry up,' she says.

We keep at it, gagging as we go. I develop a tic at the corner of my eye, like an electric switch that's trying to fire, trying to make sure the sludge doesn't come back up out of my throat. I have to concentrate on swallowing and not thinking, not even tasting it until it's all gone. I show Black Nana my dish. She scoops up the paper full of little knots of uneaten porridge and throws it in the bin.

'Good,' is her answer as she slathers grease on to my hair and weaves my plaits extra tight to stop the wispy bits escaping. My whole forehead stretches and stings where the hair pulls, but I am silent.

Black Nana walks us to the front door and then stands by the gate to watch us cross the busy road, Tracey in the crook of her arm sucking her thumb. Black Nana is tall, tall like my father, her head right up there with the lightshade and picture rail. She could see over all the hedges and brick walls and she could watch us until we disappeared if she wanted to, but when we turn round she's gone, taken Tracey inside for treats and kisses. Me and Kim hold hands and count the houses all the way to the end of the road, to the blue railings of Springfield Junior and Infant School. Thirty-four of them – tall, thin, Victorian terraces just like ours.

My teacher is Mrs Hunter and she also has plaits, but hers are long and grey and lie criss-cross across the top of her head like a dusty crown. I am smaller than everyone else and I wonder where Kim is and why I can't play with her, but Mrs Hunter makes us all sit on the floor and tells us to be quiet. She makes an announcement.

'Everyone has to have a handkerchief tomorrow. All right, children? A handkerchief that is clean and white, and you tuck it up your sleeve, like this.' She shows us her disappearing magic trick. 'And that way, we don't spread colds and coughs and diseases throughout the school.' She looks straight at me and I close my eyes to remember to tell Mom. Only Dad has handkerchiefs, big white ones that we use for dolls' sheets when we put them to bed. I'll have to ask her for one of those. I wonder what will happen to me if I spread colds and diseases to the other children.

I sit here and I sit there. I do as I am told. I follow the other children when they go outside and I follow them back into the classroom. Every single child is bigger than me. Every single boy and every single girl in my class and all the teachers and all the other children in the whole school, and I have the feeling that I will never catch them up.

I have a desk all to myself next to a girl with a funny name, Cressida. Cressida has the widest smile I've ever seen and she has freckles. She has a sister in the next year and I have a sister in the next year so we've decided to be friends. We both get a small bottle of milk with a white paper straw and have to line up to get a biscuit from Mrs Hunter. It's the best part of the day.

At four o'clock Kim is waiting for me outside school and Mom is waiting for both of us with Tracey in the big pram. It's feels like a special treat to have Mom come and collect us from school because I know that she is always at work. Cressida waves goodbye. She doesn't have the uniform on like me and my sister do and her mom has black hair in a strange haircut with a very short fringe. Cressida calls her mom 'Wendy' and I wonder if I can call my mom 'Sheila' but I know better than to ask.

Black Nana wears a headtie like a pirate and has a pirate's walk too, one leg three inches shorter than the other. She sways when she walks, her built-up shoe stamping on the lino so we always know where she is. She pulls herself up the stairs, her mighty hand on the banister, stamp, shuffle, good foot, bad foot, light foot, heavy foot, on to the landing and round the turn into the little room by the bathroom at the back of the house, her room that we must never enter.

She talks like my dad with his St Kitts accent, slow and heavy, but she doesn't talk as often as he does unless it's to tell us off or sing West Indian nursery rhymes to the one she loves. She watches us, she plays with Tracey, she cooks and she sways to and fro in her wooden chair, and walks up and down on her wooden foot.

I am scared of her. I am scared of the lump that comes out of her neck like a lemon trying to escape that makes her tip her head to the side. I am scared, but Kim is not. I think it's because she's so much older than me, two years nearly, she's a whole six years old. Even though the only thing that Black Nana and Dad and Mom all agree on is that we shouldn't answer back, Kim has found a way to answer back with her eyes and Black Nana doesn't like it.

When Black Nana tells Kim off sometimes, she doesn't say 'Yes, Nana,' like I do. She makes her eyes go narrow and just lets them do all the talking for her. Nana would like to tell Mom off and she would like to tell Mom what to do, but she can't, so she chooses the next best thing and that's Kim.

When Black Nana and Kim are staring at each other, I put my head down and won't look because the eye-to-eye conversation is worse than words. And sometimes I get caught listening and Black Nana tells me off. So when everyone's in the middle room, Kim and Black Nana and Tracey and me, I just keep still, keep quiet, make no noise. That way, I can be invisible.

Black Nana takes Tracey upstairs for her nap and sometimes she forgets to come down so me and Kim have the middle room to ourselves. We play games with the things we can find in the house, saucepans and plastic bowls. We drag the broken clothes prop in from the garden and rest it between Nana's rocking chair and the sofa. We're playing horse racing. First Kim neighs and clip-clops over the prop. Then me. Clip-clop, hop and I'm over.

'Quicker!' says Kim and we chase each other over the prop until we're screaming and I'm winning because I'm in the lead and we're pulling each other and pushing, trying to get over the jump the most times. I trip. I fall. My head hits the edge of the prop and I go down crying. Kim kneels down next to me.

'Are you all right?'

But all I do is cry and Kim says 'Shhhhhh!' but I cry loud enough to bring Nana downstairs, to bring her hand across the back of Kim's legs, slapping her three times, hard and quick. Now we're both crying and we'll wake Tracey if we're not quiet. Nana gives me a cold wet cloth for the lump on my head and I sit on the back step by the French windows next to Kim and hold her hand.

Mom comes back from work really tired and always goes to Kim first. She snuggles her first and cuddles her first because she knows about Black Nana. As soon as Mom's through the door, Kim runs up to her crying and I hear her whispering about how horrible Black Nana has been and that she got hit for doing nothing. Mom spends ages with her talking softly and quietly like Black Nana does with Tracey. Then she snuggles me and I try to make it last.

'I made a calendar at school,' I say. 'And I fell and hit the prop.' By rights, I should have left a much bigger gap between these two things and made my moment last.

'Did you?'

'Kim was in trouble with Nana and she was crying.'

Mom looks at Kim, not at me, so this is a bad move.

'And I was nice to her,' I add quickly. 'And I hurt my head.'

'Good girl,' she says, but she doesn't notice my lump because her eyes are on Tracey.

Black Nana holds the baby out for a single minute before bedtime and then Mom has to give her back. Black Nana clasps Tracey to her chest and climbs the stairs to her room. We feel a kind of triumph in her retreat. Mom is back and Black Nana can't tell us off. But we're not sure who is the boss of whom and who is winning the silent war for Tracey.

Mom takes us upstairs to her bedroom. Me and Kim are allowed to sit on the bed so she can show us what she's got in her bag. She puts her hand in and slowly, slowly, she brings it up, then 'Ta-dah!' Crisps! Smith's Crisps from the factory where she works! The bags of crisps are flat or torn, but there's always a little blue knot of salt inside that we rush to find and sprinkle on the tiny bits of crisps at the bottom.

Or she's brought home a big see-through bag of broken biscuits with pink bits of icing collected in the bottom, half a Bourbon, sticky lemon-glazed flaky pastry things and sometimes even a chocolate one with the side broken off. There are biscuits with cream in the middle, there are crumbs and corners and an inch of biscuit dust with bits of custard cream. Then there are toffee apples in funny shapes with chunks of toffee missing. We break bits off with our teeth and suck the shards until our tongues are shredded and sore.

When Mom is at home, Black Nana stays in her bed-room. We're not allowed to go in, but I peek inside when she leaves her door open. There's a little wardrobe next to a single bed and the bedspread is made of tufty stuff with little pink roses on it. There's a sort of box with a piece of wood on it that she uses for a dressing table. There are potions and pots of grease on that table, a hairbrush for hair I have never seen, different bandanas and face cream, and the whole room smells of menthol and something herby and thick. I hate it.

Sometimes, Black Nana leaves Tracey to play with us in the garden while she's pegging out the washing. We chase her little fat legs around the garden and make her squeal. We sing songs, the three of us together, and sit on her blanket in the sun. Kim is always in charge, Tracey is always happy. We all want to be with her. There are days like this, some with Mom, some without. And there are other days when Mom has Tracey all to herself, nestled into her chest, sucking her thumb or sleeping, calm and contented.

3

Good Foot, Bad Foot

I'm always on the lookout for Dad because, when he comes in, I have to be first. Sometimes he comes home early, sometimes he comes home late, so I have to keep my ears open for the exact moment that he opens the front door and then I start running.

'Patches,' he says. He's the only one who calls me Patches because I have patches of pale skin and patches of brown skin on my face where the two halves of me collide. I feel like Patches is our special word. I assume he knows that if Kim has Mom and Tracey has Black Nana, he must surely be mine. He's so tall it's hard to see his face, but as soon as the front door opens, I walk behind him up the hallway and stand by him watching him eat. His dinner is kept on a saucepan of boiling water in the kitchen so it's hot whenever he comes home. He takes it off carefully with a tea towel and puts it on the side, and sometimes, if I'm quick enough, I pass him a spoon or a fork.

He sits alone at the kitchen table and I stand next to him. He looks up from his plate sometimes as if to say 'What?' but I just smile and carry on watching him, spoon to mouth, spoon to mouth, until he has finished. I follow him into the telly room, I follow him to the bedroom. I follow him to the toilet sometimes and wait outside. When he flushes and opens the door, I am there waiting.

One day, I hear the front door open. I know it's him.

I get down from the kitchen table and run up to him. He forgets to call me Patches. He just strides down the hall, a rolled-up newspaper in his hand. Normally he taps it against his leg but this time it just hangs down loose at his side. He's walking slower than usual, tired out. He doesn't even go into the kitchen to eat, he turns left before the kitchen door and trudges up the stairs. I follow.

Right at the crook of the staircase, where I have to put two feet on each step because they're so wide, he turns suddenly and looks down at me.

'Where you going?' he snaps. It's not a question.

I put my head down and shuffle past him. 'Nowhere,' I say. I go into the big bedroom where me and my brother and sisters sleep all together and sit on the bed, ashamed and embarrassed. I won't listen for his key in the door. I won't stand and hope he doesn't burn his hand on the hot plate or rush to find a spoon and give it to him. I won't stand patient, silent, and watch him eat his dinner. I won't run up to him or wait for him to come home ever again.

I hear him go back downstairs, but I don't follow for ages. I wait and wait and hear him in the kitchen talking to Mom. I creep to the door and listen. I can hear the clink of his spoon on the Pyrex dish.

'Kim was crying when I got in, Arthur. It's happening all the time these days.'

'Mmm.'

'And do you know what Chrissie's done with the washing?' Somehow Mom makes Black Nana's name sound like she's swearing. 'Do you know what she's done? She's picked out your clothes and her clothes and Tracey's clothes. And left all the rest for me. Mine and Kim's and Mandy's. That wasn't the plan, Arthur.'

He doesn't speak. I know he's cutting the soft meat with the edge of the spoon, he's loading it on to the rice.

'She do it tomorrow,' he says.

'That's not the point.' Mom is making sure her words come out in the right order. She's making sure she's using the right voice for Dad, not too angry and not too moaning. 'She's supposed to be helping out while I'm at work, Arthur. What's she got against me? What have I done? She's living in my house.'

It's ages before he speaks. The spoon against the dish. The scrape of the chair legs on the lino. The dish in the sink. Then he speaks.

'I say she do it tomorrow. You don't hear?'

That's the voice she never answers. He's the boss of her the way Black Nana is the boss of him. I creep away, back upstairs, silent as a spider, two feet on the wide step, then all the way up.

At night, Mom comes and tucks us in. 'I don't like her,' says Kim when we're in bed, the three of us on one big double mattress, me in the middle, Tracey asleep by the wall.

'Be good,' says Mom, but I remember the voice she used for Dad and the voice he used for her. Mom's eyes say a whole page of other words that mean something else. Me and Kim can hear them loud and clear.

There are rats in the garden. They've got a nest in the broken-down shed attached to the wash house that's attached to the kitchen and Mom says we can't go outside to play even though it's sunny outside in case they bite us.

It's exciting and it's horrible and I wonder if rats can fight their way through the back wall and actually get into the kitchen and then run all over the house and then find a way to scamper upstairs and wait in dark corners or under the lino until its dark and then eat the blankets and then eat me. I think about fat rats gorged on my eyeballs and I'm scared to go to sleep.

Mom's at work. Black Nana stands over us in the middle room.

'I tired tell you keep quiet.'

But we are quiet. We are always quiet.

'Here.' She shoves a broom into Kim's hand. 'Go and clean out the shed.'

Kim doesn't move. Her eyes bulge. 'Mom said—'

'You mother here? You see you mother anywhere?'

She pushes Kim towards the French windows. 'And don't make no noise. Tracey sleeping.'

I follow my sister outside. I follow wherever she goes, always.

Kim takes the broom and we go out into the narrow passageway. When we turn round, Black Nana is watching. I know I could go inside and sit quietly invisible but Kim can't, so I have to stay with her. We stand at the latched door where the rats live. I know how dangerous this is. The broom is taller than Kim, and Kim is taller than me. The rats will be low to the ground. So when they come running out, they'll go for the nearest flesh and mine will be the first face they attack. I get ready to run.

Kim holds the broom like a sword and reaches up. As soon as she presses the latch, the wooden door swings open. We both stumble backwards, but the rats don't come. Kim takes a step inside while I stay at the door. Dust and flies hover in the thick, soupy light that falls on paint tins with buckled lids, an old suitcase, a rusty mop bucket, half a rotten table, old black boots that have curled over on themselves, splitting the sole.

Kim pokes around with the tip of the broom. Nothing. She turns and looks at me.

'Do it again,' I whisper, half dancing with terror and delight.

She pokes under the table and in the opposite corner something shifts under the coat, a scratchy sound, a rat. Suddenly, she dashes backwards and the broom stabs me in my belly.

'Owwwww!' I start to cry.

'I didn't mean it,' says Kim.

I want to say, 'I know you didn't but help me run away in case the scratchy thing comes out.' But the pain won't let me do anything except groan and cry. I'm hunched over, my belly churning in agony.

In two long, uneven strides, Black Nana is suddenly in the garden.

'What noise you making?' she says to me, at the same time snatching the broom from Kim and slamming the shed door. 'You didn't hear me say Tracey sleeping?'

'The broom hit me, Nana,' I say, deciding not to mention that's she's making more noise than me and Kim put together.

'What you say? She hit you?'

'No, Nana. The broom hit me.'

Nana turns and looks at Kim, so thoroughly my mother's child, her black, defiant eyes not turning away, not saying sorry.

'You can't hear?'

Only Kim gets the clout but we both feel it. I shut up immediately. We snivel our way back into the house and sit on the floor in the middle room, watching our grandmother sway backwards and forwards in her rocking chair, kissing her teeth and shaking her head.

'He who can't hear must feel,' she says.

Saturday morning. Mom gets up early. She stands in the kitchen and rolls up her sleeves. She's wearing trousers and a check shirt. She's bunched her hair at the back. Black Nana watches her from the doorway with Tracey on her hip.

Usually Mom doesn't look at Black Nana straight in the face, but today, as she gets ready, she meets her eye to eye and talks loud and slow like Black Nana is five years old and also a bit deaf.

'You see, when I said there were rats in the shed, Chrissie, what I meant was keep the kids away from there while I'm out at work earning enough money to put food on this table and help your son pay the bills. I don't know what they do where you come from but round here they don't send little kids to do a man's job. They don't send men half the time.'

She picks up one of Dad's cricket bats and strides over to Black Nana.

'They send women. Irishwomen.'

She turns on her heels and out of the back door and we are right behind her. Kim first, then me, then Black Nana, all of us huddled by the wash house.

'Right!' she says, like the rats can hear. She flings open the cracked wooden door to the shed and takes a step inside. Then out it all comes, flung behind her and out into the garden. Coats, boots, tins, half-table, bricks, papers, iron things, wooden things, cloth things, and then she's beating something. *Bam! Bam! Bam!*

The banging goes on forever. Mom shouting.

'Come on! Come on! I'll get you!'

The tiny shed and the fat rats are no match for the little woman from Wexford with a bellyful of resentment, and when she emerges, sweaty-faced and white-fisted, we know she has won. We can't help looking at Black Nana. There is something defeated about her.

'Look,' Mom says in triumph and gestures with her chin to my father's cricket bat. It's scratched and chipped, a deep groove down the front, black dirt, red blood. Nana turns and takes Tracey inside and leaves my mother heaving for breath, lost for words.

It's my birthday. The last I will have. I am five. A few doors away lives Jane, a big girl, eleven at least, who comes to our house to play with us. She has twinkly blue eyes and blond hair that falls all over her face and she's constantly shaking it away like a wild horse. She always wears jeans that are darned or ripped and white pumps that are scuffed and dirty, but she's posh and she's an only child and somehow we know that her scruffiness is by choice. Jane hasn't got brothers or sisters so she comes to our house so she won't be lonely. She's always happy and has great ideas about what to do, like digging up the grass and watching worms.

It's a summery day, July bright. Black Nana calls to me from the front door.

'Come, Mandy!' she says. Jane is standing there with a little box wrapped in pink paper and a big pink envelope. She holds them out to me.

'Happy birthday,' she says. 'I can't come round today because we're going on holiday. Bye.'

She skips down the path in her stripy tank top and embroidered blouse. I watch her get into one of the only cars on the street with her dad, whose hair is nearly as long as Jane's. She waves from the back seat and I wave, too. Then I run inside as fast as I can to open my present. Black Nana stands over me while I carefully pick at the Sellotape on the special wrapping paper. It's just the two of us.

Inside is a golden necklace with a little bird dangling on the chain. It's displayed on a piece of puffy cardboard and wrapped in cellophane. I don't want to unwrap it. I just want to look and touch it through the crinkly stuff with the tip of my fingers.

'Make I show you where I put it,' said Black Nana, snatching it from my hand.

'No! I want it, Nana!' I reach up but it's way too far away.

'Me put it safe,' she says, padding and stamping her way up the linoleum-covered stairs.

'But I want it, Nana,' I cry, running after her with my arms outstretched.

Pad, stamp, pad, stamp, good foot, bad foot, good foot, bad foot, up the stairs. She takes me into her forbidden room and puts her hand on the top of the wardrobe. I hear it drop.

'See it there? I look after it.'

She's so tall she can look down at the top of the wardrobe. I cannot. I just can't get up there. My precious present in the tallest tower, in the darkest place, in a witch's room where I can never return.

She prods me back down the stairs and outside into the garden.

'Go and play,' she says and I sit on the back step to wait for my mother. I tell her. She does nothing. I try Dad. He does nothing. I ask and ask and ask and then one day Black Nana grabs me by my upper arm. She pulls my face close to hers.

'It gone,' she says. 'I send it home.'

I try to do Kim's trick of telling her I hate her with only my eyes but they water over and her terrible face begins to blur. I watch her stamp away, good foot, bad foot, and I hate her even more.

Then Black Nana sets fire to Kim.

It's a Saturday and Mom's in the bath. We kneel on the bathroom floor dipping plastic bottles in Mom's bathwater and making bubbles with the bar of soap. If she's in a good mood, Mom blows gigantic bubbles which float higher and higher until they start to wobble and burst on the wall. Me and Kim try but our bubbles are small and sometimes the soap gets up your nose or in your eyes. After she gets out, Mom sits me and Kim in the bath together and she sits on the toilet with Tracey on her lap.

There's no point in bathing Tracey because Black Nana's done that already, bathed her and oiled her skin and put corn rows in her hair. It's only me and Kim who have to have our hair washed and have the comb dragged through the knots while it's still wet and twice as painful as usual.

There are no bubbles today. Mom's been in a bad mood for ages. Night after night when we've gone to bed, I can hear her talking in the next room. I can hear she's asking questions but there are no answers from Dad, only Mom's voice that sounds like she's crying.

When we're clean and fresh, she sends us downstairs. Black Nana is in the kitchen with her back to us. Her back speaks like Kim's eyes. Its stiffness and straightness tell us how she's feeling. She doesn't speak but we hear it all the same. Two words.

'Me vex.'

We sit at the kitchen table colouring in quietly while Nana cooks eggs in a frying pan, basting them over and over in boiling lard. Kim gets down to watch.

'Move,' Black Nana hisses. 'Move back before you get burn.'

But Kim is fascinated by the slow whitening of the yolk, the rhythmic flick of the spoon in the silver, shimmering oil, the slight tip of the pan, the blue-and-yellow flames that lick up the side of the cast iron and the smell of hot food.

'Move!' she says again. But it's too late. All of sudden Kim's hair is on fire, all the little curls at the top and sides are glowing, sparkling, and bits of hair are floating up to the ceiling. She screams, loud. Black Nana is quick, two slaps of her big hands and the fire is out. She grabs Kim, turns her front and back, claps again, flicks the blackening, singeing curls, but she's not quick enough. The door flies open and there is Mom with Tracey in her arms.

'What happened?'

The smell tells the tale and Kim buries her head in Mom's skirt.

'You're supposed to be looking after them, Chrissie. All of them.'

My mother's voice is trembling and quiet, not like the voice that's been moaning at Dad for weeks. Chrissie turns her back and flicks the oil over her eggs.

Black Nana doesn't wear her headtie on the day she leaves. Her hair is flat to her scalp in waves and circles. She's wearing a new coat and carrying a handbag in the crook of her arm. We watch Dad bring her suitcase downstairs and carry it outside. His face is set into a new shape, hard and sad at the same time.

Black Nana stands stiff and tall in her new coat and her uneven shoes, facing my mother in the kitchen. Tracey is cradled in my mother's arms.

'I beg you one more time, Sheila.'

I hear my mother swallow. 'No.'

'Is already two more children you have, Sheila. Two girls. And you not finished having children yet. Make me take just one. Give me Tracey.'

Nana's voice takes me by surprise. It's soft, soothing, kind. I shudder.

'I can't do that, Chrissie,' says my mother, holding Tracey tighter, taking a step backwards.

'I love the child. Let me take her. Please.'

My mother says nothing.

When Tracey begins to cry and holds her arms out, Black Nana puts her hand on the door jamb and steadies herself. One leg shakes. She looks like she might fall. She looks at me and Kim and back again at Tracey and one final begging look at my mother. Then she turns slowly, awkwardly, in the small space and walks down the hallway.

'Go and say goodbye to your grandmother,' Mom says to me. Black Nana turns slightly and, when I'm sure she can see me, I walk upstairs, stamping on each step, good foot, bad foot, all the way to the top.

Looking down from the big bedroom window, I watch her. She glances briefly up and then folds herself like a flick knife and disappears into the black cab.

After eighteen months, there's a telegram. Mom takes it to Dad and, when he opens it, he goes upstairs into the little room where his mother used to sleep.

'Don't make any noise today,' Mom says with her finger on her lips. Mom has loads of different voices – sad, happy, angry – and this voice sounds a little bit scared so we do as we are told and Dad stays in the room all day until we go to bed.

Days later, a big photograph arrives in a stiff cardboard envelope. It's Black Nana propped up in her coffin, long and narrow, surrounded by a cluster of black people, young and old, everyone in white, standing solemnly looking through the camera at us, unknown relatives, thousands of miles away, showing us how they buried the old woman and how loved she was and how many people turned out for the funeral and what my father got for his money.

Black Nana's face is sunken and hollow and everywhere there are flowers, on her chest, on her legs, on her hair. I scan the face of every little black girl in the photograph. One of them is wearing my golden necklace under her white funeral clothes.

After the photograph is put away, when everyone's forgotten about Black Nana, Mom starts talking about the new baby and how she's going to manage.

'No one here to help you now, Sheila. What you wanted, isn't it?'

Dad gets ready for work and when he leaves we hear the front door slam.

4

Play Your Cards Right

Now that Black Nana has gone and Dean has been born, Mom has to stop working at the factory. She starts cleaning other people's houses even though ours needs all the cleaning it can get. Me and Tracey and Kim are at school so Mom has to take Dean with her in his pram.

Me and Kim are happy because at least she's at home when we get in from school and we don't have to eat porridge with lumps for breakfast, but Tracey misses Black Nana's special attention and kisses.

One day, a white lady rings the bell. I'm right behind Mom when she opens the door and standing there is a woman a bit older than Mom with a posh hair set, wearing a sheepskin coat and pink nail varnish and a very big smile. She's got a raspy voice from somewhere that's not Birmingham and she talks to Mom properly, not like Mrs Kent in the corner shop, not like the neighbours who don't like us. She's kind and she looks at me and gives me a very soft pinch on my cheek. When Mom closes the door again, she's got a magazine with a drawing of happy people on the front, black people and white people all smiling and standing in a beautiful park, and all Mom does for the rest of the day is sit down and read it.

The lady comes the next day and this time she sits in the kitchen and has a cup of tea. She says her name is Stella and then tells us a great story about somewhere with tame lions and brave lambs that play together, and the lion never eats the lamb or never even wants to. Both animals love Jehovah, which is God's real name. And the picture on the front is how life will be in the future, all people living peacefully and happily together.

The other great thing is that if you believe in Jehovah, you will never, ever die. Does Mom remember the Second World War? Has she seen all the films about people being killed and bombed and starved to death in concentration camps? Well, there will be no more wars when Jehovah is in charge. Does Mom realize that there are millions of people all over the world who are starving hungry and living in poverty? Well, Jehovah will feed everyone like Jesus did with just one loaf and five fishes. And people won't die of disease and old age, people won't hate each other because of the colour of their skin, and Mom's children will grow up stroking once-wild animals and jumping around green fields with puppies and kittens while Jehovah's Witnesses build single-storey homes with white picket fences, one for everyone, no one with a bigger plot than their neighbour. Imagine that!

Mom looks at the beautiful pictures, at the black people with enough to eat living next door to white people with enough to eat, and children of all colours playing together under a blue sky and a yellow sun. There are golden fields of corn ready for an everlasting harvest, trees bending under the weight of their fruit, red apples, green apples that someone has picked until the baskets are overflowing. Not a skinny child with patchy skin in sight. All the women have neat dresses with little collars and small waists because they're not pregnant all the time. Their boy children have side partings and ironed shorts and the girl children have plaits that don't come undone with flyaway bits at the front. The women aren't tired from four jobs, and the men, in short-sleeved shirts and tool belts, are smiling mid-job, building houses in paradise for the faithful.

'Where is this?' asks Mom. She sounds like a little girl, like someone my age, full of wonder, guileless.

'Sheila,' says Stella, holding her hand, 'it's here on earth. Jehovah will bring Armageddon and cleanse the earth of all badness and wickedness, and all the people who are left will make the earth like this, like He always meant it to be.'

Stella opens the Bible at Revelation, chapter 21, verse 4. 'He will wipe every tear from their eyes,' she says. 'There will be no more death nor mourning nor crying nor pain, for the former things have passed away.'

Mom takes the Bible off her and reads it all over again out loud for everyone to hear.

'That's right,' says Stella. 'That's Jehovah's promise. All we have to do is believe in Him.'

When we go to the Kingdom Hall that Sunday, all the Jehovah's Witnesses in the congregation come up to us and say hello. There are white people and black people together, everyone wearing suits or nice clothes, there are Greek people and young people and children, and every-one smiles and says, 'Welcome!' No one looks at my mom like she's no good for having black children and so many of them so close together and no one looks at us like we're dirty. We are on our best behaviour and so is Mom. She's speaking slowly and clearly, her in-control-of-her-family voice, ready to learn and bend to the will of God if only for everlasting life and a long rest. Someone gives us a songbook so we can join in and a Bible so we can look up the scriptures, and we sit all together on one row and listen to the man at the front who talks for ages about paradise and how to get there.

When it's over, Stella takes us home in her car and says she'll come back next week. And she does. She comes for weeks and weeks, and every time she brings someone new with her who says the same thing as Stella, who confirms all the scriptures and all God's promises, and paradise gets closer and closer the more Mom believes in it.

Then Mom gets baptized at the big assembly in London and people start to call her 'Sister'. She learns all the rules and all the things she has to do to actually get to paradise, all the studying and preaching and not smoking and not fornicating, nor swearing, nor stealing or even thinking about stealing, and giving a little bit of money if you can afford it and remembering the widow's mite if you can't, and making sure that everyone knows you're a Jehovah's Witness because otherwise you are like Peter who denied Jesus (his best friend), and grabbing every single opportunity to witness to people, even in the most unusual circumstances like on the bus or at the park, and then answering questions at the Kingdom Hall by putting up your hand and reading out a scripture, and attending every single meeting no matter what the weather, good or bad, and deciding whether you want to be wheat or you want to be chaff because the chaff gets blown away but the wheat isn't, and women not wearing trousers and men always wearing a suit and tie and never ever having a beard because that would make them look like hippies, but a moustache is OK, and women not teaching men but knowing their place in God's order of things, and children being respectful to their parents and obedient in all things, remaining virgins until marriage and only marrying another Jehovah's Witness, and cutting out any bits of yourself that felt like they were turning you into a homosexual, which is an abomination unto the Lord, and remembering not to talk to anyone who used to be a Jehovah's Witness but got themselves disfellowshipped, which means they can't be talked to or looked at or included in anything because that is a kindness to them and makes them miss you and eventually drives them back into the flock, and if ever you were in any doubt about anything whatsoever there is a scripture in the Jehovah's Witness special edition of the Bible that can tell you how to behave or what to do or what to believe and from now on you will never, ever be in any doubt about anything as long as you live. Play your cards right, keep the rules and you will live forever.

Of course, it is important to remember that Jehovah made us with free will. Maybe you don't want to keep the rules and maybe you know other card games which don't involve the Bible. If that's the case and you don't want to live forever, there is also something waiting for you. For the liars and thieves and people who watch *Top of the Pops* instead of going to the meeting and people who accept birthday cards and people who want to have sex with their boyfriend or girlfriend or boyfriend and girlfriend and people who think hymns sound nice and anyone who is Catholic or Muslim or Sikh, Christadelphian, Methodist, Baptist, Mormon, Seventh Day Adventist, Church of England, Hindu, Jew, atheist, Scientologist, Buddhist or just plum not interested, there is a terrible death waiting for them. They will die at Armageddon when God brings his righteous judgement on all the evil people in the world with earthquakes and floods and fires and death and destruction.

There isn't long to wait. No. The end will come in 1975 when I am fifteen, in a few years' time, before I leave school, before I grow up. That's the date that Jehovah's specially chosen people have worked out by using a bit of the Book of Daniel and some of the scriptures in Revelation and multiplied one by the other and come out with 1975. Or thereabouts. The date has been set by Jehovah and that's the truth. All we have to do is be good and wait it out.

5

In the Book

Me, Kim and Tracey are all in the Juniors now. Dean is in the Infants. We go to school together, holding hands, being extra careful at the crossing because we live on the 91 bus route. Springfield Road is so narrow that when two buses meet they have to pull in tight to the pavement and inch by in order to pass one another. Sometimes, when they get close, the bus drivers will stop for a few minutes, lean on their open windows and chat like neighbours over a garden fence. Then the upstairs passengers will look at us in our bedrooms, in our front gardens, and someone will wave and we wave back.

The bottom of Springfield Road starts in Stratford Road, Sparkhill, the main road that runs south from the centre of Birmingham right out to Stratford-upon-Avon, through little outlying towns and villages. It's white and respectable and filled with working-class people who dream of Hall Green and Solihull and Henley-in-Arden and maybe even Stratford itself. Our bit of Stratford Road has a long parade of shops: the butcher, the baker, the barber, the sweetshop, the hardware store, the shoe shop, the bank and post office, the launderette and Woolworths. But once you turn off by the bank and up Springfield Road, it gets posher, it gets semi-detached, it gets detached.

The very top of our road meets Wake Green Road, which travels all the way into Moseley Village where huge

Victorian mansions sit back behind gravel drives far from the pavement, villas with coach houses and turrets and acres of gardens for the children of barristers and solicitors, professors and surgeons. But we live slap bang in the middle of Springfield Road in a narrow Edwardian terraced house, our garden backing on to the playing fields of the local secondary school and beyond that the grammar school where the clever boys from Moseley learn how to take after their fathers.

Each row of five or six houses is served by an entry that leads from the street to the back of the garden. Each house has a little front garden and a wooden gate and each house does its best to be respectable with net curtains, a flowerpot, a brass knocker.

Across our road, on the corner of Passey Road, there are two shops, a newsagent and Kent's, the general grocers, where you can buy things on tick or, as Mrs Kent called it, 'in the book'.

Mrs Kent wears cat's-eyes glasses under a head of luxurious sandy curls, flattened into place by a hairnet. She and Mr Kent wear white overalls when they're in the shop like they're dispensing medicine or about to give you a filling. The shop has huge weighing scales and so much food that the shelves reach from floor to ceiling and Mr Kent has an exciting claw on a stick that he uses to bring down the bleach or the candles. The shop is a hallowed, neat place where you don't make a noise, where you wait your turn, where there is a kind of order I see nowhere else.

When Mom's in the shop buying stuff, Mrs Kent always asks her if she wants to pay or if she wants it 'in the book'.

She knows the answer because, before Mom can speak, Mrs Kent bends down and takes a big navy-blue ledger from under the counter. She puts her skinny finger in her mouth for a little spit and turns the pages slowly, a neatly annotated leaf for each neighbour who can't afford to pay, until she gets to our pages. She goes down each entry with the tip of a sharp red pencil until she finds the total.

'So that's today's date, 4th May, and it's another two shillings and ninepence. That makes ... Let me see ... Five shillings and thruppence exactly. Shall we say next week, Mrs O'Loughlin?'

My mother wears the beatific smile of a woman who has temporarily mislaid a bulging purse and says in a loud, clear voice with an English accent, 'Lovely, thank you. Yes, next week, Mrs Kent.'

She picks up the sugar and bread and the bit of ham that she can't afford and takes her time walking out and crossing the road in case the Kents are watching her, standing in front of their neat shelves in their spotless white coats and wondering when they'll get their money.

Mr and Mrs Kent don't like us to be in the shop unless we have already made up our minds. We can't go in to ogle at the sweets and see which look best and decide on the spot. We can't look at anything for too long and we can't get too close to the counter. We have to go in, say what we want and pay.

On Saturdays, Dad gives us pocket money. It is rationed by our years. Kim gets two shillings and sixpence or half a crown, I get two shillings, Tracey gets one and six, Dean gets a shilling and Karen gets sixpence. I always give Tracey three pennies so we both have one and nine.

We rush to Kent's but we have to wait outside for one another because they don't like us to be cluttering the shop up with our sticky brown fingers.

I am worried about not knowing what I want and not being fast enough with my choice. I think hard throughout the one-minute journey to the shop. The main thing is to make sure I get sweets that will last. Sherbet Dip Dabs can take ages to disappear because you have both the little lolly and the sugary powder; Flying Saucers just melt on your tongue in seconds so they are out; but sweet cigarettes, Fruit Salads, Black Jacks and gobstoppers could see me through most of the day and into the evening.

Mr Kent uses tongs to select the sweets and drops them into a white paper bag that he twists at the top. When I've finished, he just holds out his hand for the money like I've been counting along and know exactly what I've spent, and he's right. I have. I give him one and six and keep thruppence back for another day. He never says thank you, just watches me leave and hold the door open for my sister.

When Asian families begin to move into the area, when the other corner shop is bought by Mr Sanghera and his wife and he starts selling sanitary towels and tinned carrots next to the *News of the World* and penny chews, the Kents pull down the blinds on the shop windows and retire to their back rooms and the flat above. The shop door is never open and the tinkling bell is quiet; they leave by the garden gate and walk arm in arm to St Christopher's Church every Sunday in their matching tweed coats, slightly crumpled, slightly lost. In half a year they sell up to Mr and Mrs Khan, who open a tailor's and a mender, selling paraffin, Pakistani sweets and bolts of jewel-bright satin.

But, usually, Mom does her shopping down on Stratford Road, always bits of things – a quarter of a pound of this and a small packet of that, the last loaf of bread, the dented tin – never big bags of stuff, never, ever enough. There's an Irish shop a bus journey away and sometimes, if we're going to Nan's, Mom buys funny sausages and pink biscuits and bread that tastes like cake, crumbly and dark, because she can't expect Nan to feed us all without moaning.

If she walks down to the shops on a Saturday just before closing, she can get things cheap: apples with marks and bruises, cold meat that won't last the weekend, bread they couldn't sell. She comes home and makes us strange sandwiches or cuts the scabs off the apples with a potato peeler.

'Don't look like that. There's nothing wrong with them. We used to live off these.'

She never cuts enough off. There's always a bit of brown or a horrible soft bit, mushy and weeping.

'I'm not hungry, Mom.'

'Eat it.'

And I do because I am.

6

Happiness is the Shiny Thing

Cressida is now my best friend and I love her. She's funny and smiley and she's eight in April and I'm eight in July so she's older than me and she is very posh. Her house isn't as big as ours but it's better in every way, with matching furniture and pictures on the wall. Every room has carpet and heaters, and when they have something to eat, Cressida's mom puts a tablecloth down first with knives and forks and spoons. Cressida has her own bedroom and her own toys. She calls her mom 'Wendy', she calls her dad 'Alan', and I am jealous to the marrow. When I go to her house after school or on a Saturday, she never, ever has to tidy up and Wendy tells her to be more like me, polite like me, to help with the chores and do as she is told and be respectful like I am to my parents. She doesn't know I'd give a healthy limb to have a week at Cressida's warm house with its ever-lasting smell of roast dinners and hot chocolate.

Cressida's parents are different to mine. Not only do they let her use their first names but she can answer back as well, she can refuse to do things, she hasn't got jobs around the house, she never gets told off and when her dad comes in, he notices her and kisses the top of her head and then he says hello to me.

And then Alan kisses Wendy and starts talking to every-one. He doesn't get special treatment, he's not the boss of things. He has to wait for his dinner and go upstairs and get changed, and when he's talking anyone can talk over him or not listen at all. Alan looks like a newscaster in a shirt and tie and a suit, but sometimes when he's not at work on Saturdays, he wafts around the house in a red-and-yellow kimono and listens to records over and over again in their plush front room.

'Listen. Just listen,' he says and lifts the needle off the record and places it back at the beginning of the track. Cressida wanders off to her mother in the other room, but I watch Alan smoking his long white cigarette, barefooted, his white legs and ankles uncovered, strange-looking with-out his glasses on and his neat side parting.

'Listen,' he says, 'The Beatles,' and he plays a record about tangerine trees and kaleidoscope eyes.

'What do you think of it, Mandy?'

It's not important to answer Alan like I have to with my own father. It's not important to know the difference between the question that will get you into trouble and the question that requires immediate, evasive and non-incriminating answers.

'Marmalade skies,' I say, focusing on the food.

'Yes, just imagine that,' he says and takes a very long suck on his cigarette, and when he talks, the smoke comes out with the words at the same time. '*Lucy in the sky with diamonds* or is it *Mandy in the sky with diamonds*, eh? Will you have diamonds when you grow up?'

I look at him and smile because I know it's not a real question.

He comes close and whispers. 'Diamonds aren't really important,' he says and pats me on my head. 'Happiness is the shiny thing.'

There's a moment when we smile at each other and I love Alan Dent with all my heart.

All of a sudden, the door flies open. It's Cressida. 'No!' she says. 'She's my friend, Alan, not yours.'

Alan makes a little bow and says, 'I do apologize.'

'Good,' she answers with supreme indifference. 'We're going upstairs to play.' I turn back to look at Alan in case I have to say sorry as well but he's turned back to the window, puffing his cigarette and singing.

One Saturday morning, Cressida and me are in her bedroom. Her room isn't cold and her bed isn't damp. She has a whole room to herself and every day Wendy makes her bed and tucks the blankets in. There's carpet on the floor and curtains with a bear pattern. This is a room I could sleep in. I wouldn't stay awake for hours, scared to move my leg from the slither of warmth I have made. I wouldn't lie awake until the whole house has gone quiet and the buses have stopped rumbling up the street. I would sleep and have nice dreams and, in the morning, Wendy would call me down for a massive breakfast and Alan would kiss us both goodbye.

Wendy has to knock on Cressida's door if she wants to come in.

'Yes?' says Cressida.

Wendy brings in a tray of sandwiches and pop. There are chocolate biscuits in blue wrappers, there are two packets of crisps.

'No, Wendy!' says Cressida. 'We're playing! We're not hungry!'

I watch the retreat of the tray, Wendy shaking her head while my stomach twangs with wanting and constriction. I want to tell her I had no breakfast, lunch is only a possibility and dinner is in doubt. We are playing with dolls, dressing and undressing them in actual Barbie outfits, sitting them at the actual, special Barbie table and chairs, and trying out Barbie bags and Barbie shoes and brushing their nylon hair with the pink Barbie brush.

'My Barbie's hungry,' I say.

'Mine isn't,' says Cressida.

I wonder what I could do to make Wendy stay with the tray or if I could be brave enough to ask for something to eat. Cressida is really kind and she won't mind and she won't make me ashamed, but I know what my father would say. Never ask a stranger for food. Cressida never asks for food when she comes to my house, but then again, Cressida is never hungry.

'Who is that boy?' she asks.

'What boy?'

'The coloured boy who comes to your house after school.'

'Oh, that's Conrad,' I say. 'Mom looks after him.'

'Every day?'

'Yes.'

'You've always got people to play with,' she says. 'You're lucky. I wish I lived at your house.'

I think of our house, crammed with children and Mom and Dad and now the semi-permanent fixture of Conrad, shy and quiet and older than all of us. Sometimes Mom collects him after school and he comes home with us and stays until his mom comes and collects him and takes him away. His mom is black and neat and always seems to wear a headscarf tied under her chin. She doesn't come in, just waits on the doorstep, and then Conrad is gone. He hardly ever talks, but he plays with us and stays out of Dad's orbit, and we've got used to his silent ways.

There are six Junior School classrooms spaced evenly around a square assembly hall. There is a little stage and doors to the Headmaster's Office and to the playground. Each class has a bench outside and from time to time each bench supports a naughty child, sometimes crying, sometimes kicking the floor or picking a scab or wandering, worst of all, around the hallway and looking through the half-glass doors. There's a sort of atrium above where the sun comes in, pink and yellow through stained glass, making shapes on the wooden floor, little blocks of mahogany in elaborate shapes, worn and slippery, smelling of wax and leaves and teachers' perfume.

Mr Hargreaves is our teacher, and he was in the war. He wears a double-breasted suit in dull navy with many, many buttons, every single one fastened into place around his trim little body. His teeth are long and mustard-coloured with gaps between each one and his shoes shine like my dad's, better even, which is a difficult thing to believe.

He talks about the war like it happened down the road last week and was won by him and his unit, his lads, the boys, us and them, Gerrys everywhere.

'Showed 'em, we did.'

He talks about death in casual, throwaway anecdotes, this one who got a snakebite, that one who bled to death, another one with no legs but 'no time to stop, lads'. He says 'Ha-ha' by way of punctuation, little joiners between his long, technical sentences.

'. . . strategic targets . . . ha-ha . . . impossible but necessary . . . ha-ha . . . four hundred of us and yet still . . . ha-ha.'

After lunch every Friday we have to learn marching songs. He uses his thumb and forefinger for tempo, an imaginary baton under his arm.

Some talk of Alexander and some of Hercules
Of Hector and Lysander and such great men as these
But of all the world's brave heroes, there's none that
  can compare
Let's tow, row, row, row, row, row to the British
  Grenadiers.

'Oh yes,' he says at the beginning of his long remem-brances, 'oh yes, you lot will never know what it is to be afraid. Ha-ha. Twenty-three years ago. Lest we forget. We saved you from tyranny. Ha-ha. Paid with our lives.'

He stands stock-still but definitely not dead under the high windows that open at the pull of a rope, hands gripping one another behind his back, gripping and ungripping, over and over. A splodge of sun lands on his bald head and he stays there until the noise of fidgeting and scraping chairs drags him back from the bridges of Holland, from the beaches of Normandy.

'Now, then!'

He marches to his desk and writes 'Geography' on the board in a looping, beautiful hand. '*Geo*, meaning earth. Study of the earth and how we live on it. What is it?'

Indistinct mumbling.

'What is it, O'Flaherty, boy?'

'John graffi.'

'Oh dear, dear me. Even in Ireland they study the earth, don't they? The bog at least. Ho-ho!' he laughs. 'What do they teach you over there?'

Dermot O'Flaherty has six brothers and one sister who is shockingly beautiful. They all live in a little house off Stratford Road with their mother, tiny Bridie O'Flaherty, and Tommy O'Flaherty, who everyone knows is not to be angered and who talks about politics to everyone who will listen. Mom says he's the most intelligent man she's ever known and it's a shame he drinks so much. Sometimes, he stops her on the street and they talk in their own accent and maybe another Irish neighbour will join in and I listen to the way they speak, whispery from Wexford and growling from Cork and Dublin accents with the half-joke at the end. They talk and talk and put the world to rights. Tommy O'Flaherty could have been a politician, Mom says when he's gone, he could have been a teacher or a professor, but he's Irish and we're Irish and the Irish have to work for a living.

Mr Hargreaves is standing up and shouting at Dermot.

'It is geo-graphy, you stupid boy! Greek! *Geo!* The earth! Greek! *Graph!* To write! Geography! Say it! All of you! Say it!'

'Geo-graphy.'

'And what is geography? Hands up. Anyone?'

Diane Jackson, who sits right at the front of the class with her flat face as round and white as a full moon, answers. Of course she does. Diane Jackson is posh and lives on Woodlands Road, right across from Mr Hargreaves, and everyone knows he passes her the answers on his way to school so she can be the best.

'Learning about different countries, sir.'

'That's right, Diane. Good girl. Now then . . .'

The creamy light from the high windows falls on my desk. It's as warm and soft as a baby's blanket. Sometimes when people start talking the sound feels far away and I can think whatever I like. My head feels heavy on my neck and the whole world feels like the time in between waking and sleeping when everything is quiet. The sunshine pours like golden syrup over the ink-stained wood, over my hands, paints my jumper the palest green and makes shimmering patterns on the parquet floor, dull and dark brown . . . oh, look, tiny, tiny flakes of dust dance in the brightness and I try to follow one, just one, as it floats and curls, buoyed up by the thick breath of thirty children or puffs of wind from the gaps in the window . . . if I got really, really close to one of the bits of dust, maybe I could see what they are made of, maybe they are tiny petals or bits of pollen that bees collect or maybe they might be something to eat, like manna from heaven . . . but they don't sparkle or shine so, no, they're not made of gold, but then some of them are nearly invisible, so small and . . . are they getting smaller . . . no, not smaller, just floating away and up towards the . . . maybe they are tiny little butterflies, maybe they are special, clever, teeny-tiny birds, magic birds with . . . but they're so small that—

'DREAMO!'

My heart stops. Mr Hargreaves's face is next to mine. He blocks out the whole world. I can see right between the gaps in his teeth and where they meet his pink gums there is a crescent of yellowy brown. His face is raw from a savage shave, the dome of his head is enormous, round and damp with sweat, bulging from the tight knot of his regimental tie, the over-starch of his collar.

'DREEEAAAMMMO,' he sings, 'DREEEAAAMMMO!' and Pamela Pearson beside me snorts. Pamela Pearson sits at the desk next to mine. Somehow, she has positioned herself between me and Cressida and wants to be her best friend, she wants to take Cressida away from me. She lives nearer to Cressida than I do and she has miles of red hair that she wears in a ponytail with a green velvet ribbon. When she walks anywhere, when she runs at playtime, she makes sure her ponytail swings from side to side, long, thick, silky like a mermaid's, like a princess's. She's not pretty and she wears glasses and she's not clever and if she bumps into you she never says sorry and she always squeezes herself out of the door before anyone else and once she pushed a smaller girl over in the playground and pretended someone else did it. Everything about Pamela Pearson is horrible except she's got the best hair in the school.

'Dreeeaammmo,' she whispers.

Mr Hargreaves raps on my desk with his fountain pen. 'What is the earth made of, little Dreamo?'

His purple lips spread tight across his face in a smile that isn't a smile at all.

'Come on now, Dreamo. You were listening, weren't you? Not off with the fairies again? What did I say would happen if you kept daydreaming? What did I say?'

'I don't know, sir.' Everyone is listening, Cressida and clever Diane and Pamela Pearson and all the boys and all the children who pay attention and are never caught thinking about other things.

'What?'

'I'd be in trouble, sir,' I say and wonder if he will forgive me because I have remembered at last.

He pulls me out of my chair by my arm. 'And, little Miss Fuzzy Wuzzy, trouble is visited upon you this day.'

He marches me in a soldier's grip to the door of the classroom. He pulls open the door and throws me down on the wooden bench. I have been here before. I will be here again.

On Monday mornings, we have Music. Every song with Mr Hargreaves is an opportunity for patriotism.

'And second verse!' he bellows, pointing with his finger, his neck straining out of his shirt.

The door opens to the headmaster. We would stand but we are standing already for Jerusalem, God and country.

'This is lovely,' he says. He's a tall man with wiry hair barely contained by the tracks of his comb. He has forced a reluctant parting between his mouse-brown waves, a deep cleft in a brown, wiry sea of curls. Normally, we only see him for assembly, so this is a special moment.

'Sit, sit, class. Ah, Mr Hargreaves, may I borrow you?'

I turn to speak to Cressida but she's already talking to Pamela Pearson. Cressida starts laughing and Pamela's spiteful eyes twinkle and stare at me. I twist back in my seat and face the blackboard. The whispering behind me intensifies and I hear the words 'birthday party' and I sink lower in my seat. Cressida is inviting Pamela to her eighth birthday party. I will not be there. Birthday parties are not allowed by Jehovah's Witnesses and when we have birthdays in our house you have to not mention it or tell anyone because it's just like any other day and, anyway, a birthday is just an occasion for selfishness when you draw attention to yourself. When we ask Mom why we can't go to birthday parties and why we can't have presents, she says there are only two birthdays mentioned in the Bible, John the Baptist's and King Herod's, and on both occasions good people died. So birthdays are bad and I can't buy my best friend a present and, even if I could, I have no money and that means Pamela will take Cressida off me and they will become best friends and leave me out forever.

Pamela kicks the side of my desk while she giggles with Cressida and I have to pretend I don't notice.

Mr Hargreaves returns. We stand.

'Right! Sit! Class 3C, you have been chosen to sing the Harvest Festival song "We Plough the Fields and Scatter", which we shall learn! We will not disgrace Springfield Junior School, nor those sacred words, nor ourselves, but first "Jerusalem"!

He taps the blackboard. 'From here!'

And was Jerusalem builded here,
Among these dark Satanic mills?

I think of all the Satanic mills in England and wonder where they are. Mills are factories and there are loads of factories on the way to the Kingdom Hall on Stratford Road, and I wonder about Satan, the Great Deceiver, and what he does in those factories and what he's making. Bombs to kill Jehovah's people and bad books that tell people that Jehovah's Witnesses aren't the only true Christians, and things that help people have blood transfusions, which is against God's Law. And then I suddenly realize I'm singing a hymn and my heart trembles.

Mr Hargreaves leads us ever onward to the beautiful climax and my heart swells with the music and the poetry and I love it. I cannot stand up and tell the teacher that I can't sing it any more, that I'm a Jehovah's Witness and my mom wants me to walk out and sit on the bench. I don't want sixty eyes on my back, mocking, pitying, not understanding.

Mr Hargreaves knocks his desk with his knuckles. 'Verse three! I say again. Verse three!'

> *Bring me my bow of burning gold:*
> *Bring me my arrows of desire:*
> *Bring me my spear: O clouds, unfold!*
> *Bring me my chariot of fire.*

I will die for my cowardice. I will die for the beautiful words. I will die for loving 'Jerusalem'.

In the afternoon, we have Maths and Spellings. Spelling tests are easy and so is composition. Maths is harder. Somehow, Mr Hargreaves makes maths into impossible stories.

'John, Bob, Peter and Derek go on a school trip. The cost of the trip is £10. Bob pays twice as much as Derek and John. Peter pays £1.'

I know all about Peter's problem. Peter is poor, that's why he's only paying £1. I feel sorry for Peter and hope no one finds out that he hasn't paid the same as everyone else. I wonder if Peter is going to go on the trip at all because he won't have any spending money. Peter probably lives in a house like ours where there's never enough food and his parents always talk about how much things cost.

Mr Hargreaves bangs my desk as he walks past. 'Write!' he bellows and the whole afternoon goes like that, very short, bewildering stories without nearly enough information that somehow have a number for an answer. Gary has more chocolate than Linda who has three cakes. Derek has apples, Barbara has pears and a dog.

I don't try, that's what Mr Hargreaves says when he reads my answers. He says that I only like the easy things and I wonder why that's so wrong.

For spellings, Mr Hargreaves sits at his desk reading out random words while Pamela Pearson pinches my arm as usual.

'Show me,' she says.

I look at Mr Hargreaves, who is reading the words off a page. I don't answer Pamela Pearson. I shuffle away from her and carry on.

'Develop,' says Mr Hargreaves.

I write it down and Pamela Pearson leans over. The pinch is painful.

'Wog,' she whispers. I pretend I can't hear her and close my eyes to think whether occur might have two 'c's or one.

'Blackie!' she hisses.

I look at her. 'Spell it,' I say.

'W.O.G.,' she says.

I smile. 'You can't spell "blackie", can you?'

This time when she pinches me, she turns the skin between her fingers and I gasp. Mr Hargreaves looks up and catches me.

'Finished?' he says. 'No? Then get on with it and stop disturbing Pamela.'

Months of pinching and prodding from Pamela Pearson, weeks of pinches and pokes into my back while I do nothing, has come to this.

'I'm going to get you,' I say to her and she returns an ugly smile that suits her perfectly.

It's four o'clock and we meet outside in the playground. The word has gone round. There's going to be a scrap. Half of our class is there, and children from other classes. Boys as well. There's a big circle of children all waiting for something to happen. Pamela Pearson is bigger than me and I already know that she's got a massive head start on violence but, before I can change my mind, Cressida pushes me and someone pushes Pamela Pearson at the same time. We clash together and it starts.

The nasty white girl who lives on the posh street is no match for a bullied black girl who's going to die anyway, who's tired of being the smallest in the class, the hungriest in the class, who probably won't bring the right tins for the Harvest Festival, who is losing her best friend, who wants Barbie hair and Barbie clothes and birthday presents, who's bored in class and bored at home and bored at the meetings that go on for hours even when it's dark, even when it's cold outside, who has bruises on her arm and bruises on her back.

Pamela Pearson's perfect hair is her downfall. I pull it down and smack her hard in her face, once, twice, three times, until there is blood. I back off. I feel the blood in my veins and the coursing vindication of revenge and I'm scared. She starts to cry, stumbling into the crowd as I pick up my satchel and walk home.

My father is leaving for work when I open the front door. He looks at me.

'What happen?' He shoves me into the kitchen. 'Sheilo! Sheilo! Look.'

Only then do I see the blood on my hands, a strange black lump on my wrist, and feel the scratch across my neck. My mother pulls my cardigan off.

'Who did this?'

She turns me round and examines me back and front.

'Where are they?'

Her face is white and trembling.

'Was it someone at school? Where did it happen? Who did it?'

'It was Pamela Pearson, Mom,' I say and begin to cry.

'That same girl?'

'Yes.'

'The stupid one that keeps copying off you?'

'Yes.'

'When? Where did this happen?'

'Just now in the playground.'

My father comes up close to me. He has to bend from his waist. 'You hit her?'

'Yes, Dad.'

'Who see you?'

'Everybody.'

He stands straight and rolls his newspaper tight.

'Good,' he says and whistles his way back down the hall, opens the front door and is gone.

7

Give Me a Kith

One day, we come home from school and Dad is in the kitchen.

'Your mother is in hospital,' he says, bending over the cooker, stirring something in a saucepan. 'The baby coming.'

He hardly looks at us. 'Sit down. You hungry? Course you is hungry. Sit down.'

We watch him like he's a magician as he tips in little drops of vanilla essence, stirring, then some nutmeg and stirring and then a pour of evaporated milk, and again he does it and again until he's happy.

'Good,' he says. 'Kim, put out the plates. Mandy, get the spoons.'

We run around the kitchen trying to find clean dishes and lay everything out on the table.

'Corn porridge,' he says, like we haven't guessed, like we haven't smelt the grated nutmeg from the front door and the hot, sugary cauldron of delight.

He pours it, thick and golden, on to the waiting plates, where it oozes out right to the rim. He sprinkles it with even more sugar and a final slick of evaporated milk around the edge.

'Careful,' he says as he backs away. 'Eat slow. It hot.'

Slow is impossible where corn porridge is concerned. The cooler it gets the more it solidifies. There is a perfect moment when it's cool enough to eat, sweet, molten, fragrant, and we plunge our spoons in over and over until it's all gone, then run our fingers over the tundra of the empty plate and lick it clean.

Dad watches us eat with his arms folded. He looks like the big statue of Nebuchadnezzar in the *Babylon the Great* book, the one who was toppled by the ball of stone that means the end of the world is coming. But Dad doesn't believe all that and we don't have to talk about paradise and lions and lambs, we don't have to go to the meetings and walk all the way down Woodlands Road in the rain when Mom isn't here. When we look up, he is smiling.

'Bit left. You want it?'

He dollops the last of it on to our plates. 'It eat good, don't it?'

That's how we eat for the three days that Mom is away. Dad takes the days off work and feeds us. He makes Johnny Cakes and saltfish, broiled pork steaks, souse with pigs' trotters in vinegar and lemon, rice and gunga peas and chicken that takes hours to brown in a big iron pot. He lets us watch the telly and then sends us to bed. He doesn't pull our hair and grease it with pink gunk from a plastic jar, dragging the brush through the knots so hard our necks jerk backwards and we get it poked back into position. He doesn't weave plaits so tight that it's hard to blink and our foreheads sing a stinging song all the way to school. He doesn't do our hair at all and we have to pick the fluff and dust out and brush the flyaway curls back into place all on our own. But the house rattles without Mom in it and we wander its rooms more than usual.

On the last day when I come in from school he sends us straight upstairs to their bedroom. The room is hot and Mom's in bed.

'Go and wash your hands,' she whispers.

When I come back, I notice a new crib next to her and in it is a new, small brown baby. Me, Kim and Tracey crowd around it. Dean is sitting on the bed next to Mom. Kim is first to hold it and then it's my turn.

'Hold your arms like this,' she says and lowers the bundle on to my lap. The baby has black hair but the rest of it is hidden under a white blanket that also looks brand new.

'Her name's Karen,' Mom announces and then she quickly takes her away to give to Tracey. When we've all had a hold, we have to go downstairs and sit quietly in the telly room. We can hear Mom and Dad talking in the bedroom in whispery voices so the new baby doesn't cry. Later, Dad brings down new nappies that need to be washed before they can go on the new baby's bum. And then new baby clothes in white and yellow and pink, and a new rattle for the new baby, and lots of other new things that we aren't allowed to touch.

Dad forgets to make our porridge that evening. He stays upstairs with the new baby and the children that they already have are hungry when they go to bed.

Me and Tracey are playing in the big room upstairs. We jump from bed to bed and then on to the little table with four wheels, once on to the floor, up on to the chair, off the chair and on to the bed and round again. It's our best game.

Downstairs, we can hear the radio. Mom's in the kitchen with the baby and Dean, and Kim is somewhere with a book. Mom always has music on wherever she is and her voice floats upstairs and we join in.

We don't know the rest of the words so we sing it over and over, chasing each other around the bedroom.

'I'm Mr Tambourine Man!'

'No, *I'm* Mr Tambourine Man!'

And then I land on the table with four wheels and the song changes.

'I can't get no satisfaction! I can't get no satisfaction!'

I'm dancing on the table and there's no room for Tracey so I stay there and raise my arms in the air. She's trying to climb up, but I keep shuffling my feet so there's no room for her. She keeps asking but all I do is sing louder and louder.

'I can't get no, nah, nah, nah, satisfaction!'

When the table starts to tip, I'm not worried. It's done this before and I just land on the bed and bounce off again. But this time when I go down I hit my mouth on the bedstead and everything feels funny. I lie there for a little while because something's happened to my lips and I can't talk. I turn round to Tracey to tell her, but when I open my mouth she screams and runs downstairs.

I run after her with the funny taste in my mouth and when I get to the bottom of the stairs by the kitchen Mom is standing there with a horrible look on her face. She grabs me and calls for Kim.

'Run over the road to Marge. Tell her ring an ambulance. Tell her to come quick.'

I keep looking at Mom, wondering why she wants an ambulance, but I can't talk because of the thing in my mouth.

'Don't worry, love,' Mom says, but her face is whiter than usual. Tracey is staring at me and Dean is sucking his dummy and holding Mom's hand and we all stand up by the front door with the new baby in the pram.

Mom's voice is trembly. She bends down and opens my mouth and puts her finger in and tells me to swallow. When Mom takes her finger out of my mouth, it's covered in blood. Everything is wrong. And now my tongue is beginning to hurt, but every time I go to speak nothing comes out.

'Don't worry, love,' she says again, 'we'll be at the hospital soon,' and then I realize the hospital is for me and I start to cry. I want to say 'no' but it comes out wrong and every time I swallow it's getting worse and worse. I put my arms up for Mom to pick me up, but she's putting Dean at the other end of the pram to the new baby Karen and pushing it out on to the street.

'Tracey, run and get my bag.'

Tracey runs inside and comes back. Then Marge is trotting across Springfield Road with her rollers in a headscarf and a cigarette in her mouth. Ken pulls up outside in his Rover.

Mom's crying and I'm crying and Marge takes one look at me and covers her mouth with her hand.

'Sweet bloody Jesus!'

'It's her tongue, Marge.'

Marge grabs Mom by the arm and shoves her towards the car.

'Don't wait for the ambulance, Sheila. Get in! Ken'll drive you. In! In! I'll stop with the kids.'

I sit on Mom's lap and Ken zooms away. Mom spends the whole journey putting her finger in my mouth all the time and telling me to swallow. She makes little yelps like a dog when I tell her I can't do it.

At the hospital I'm on a wheely bed like the table I fell off but much bigger. And then all of a sudden I'm in a very white room under hundreds and hundreds of the brightest lights in the world and loads of nurses are holding my arms and legs and my head. Mom is nowhere to be seen.

The thing that really makes me scream is the doctor trying to get his whole hand in my mouth. Someone is holding my chin and he keeps sticking something into my tongue and pulling it. My screams are coming from my belly and my nose because there's no room to let it out of my mouth. When he's finished, one of the nurses gives me a pink drink and tells me not to swallow but to spit it out, but I can't swallow anything because I'm crying so much.

Ken is still there with Mom. They take me home after ages and ages and Mom sleeps with me all night in Dean's bed. She keeps stroking my hair and asking me if I'm all right and I just nod.

In the morning, Mom helps me come downstairs because my legs feel funny as well as my mouth. She sits me at the kitchen table and Dad shakes his head.

'What you was doing on the table, eh?'

'Don't make her talk, Arthur! Look at her lips, look at her mouth.' She pulls my chin and I have to open my big swollen lips and show him my tongue.

He winces and looks away.

'Six stitches, Arthur. They said she nearly bit it off altogether.'

She opens the fridge and takes out a block of ice cream in a blue-and-white-striped packet. She cuts a massive slice and puts it on a saucer in front of me with a teaspoon. Tracey and Kim are open-mouthed.

'The doctor says she can only have ice cream and soft food. And she has to rinse her mouth with salt three times a day. And take that,' she says, pointing to a bottle of medicine on the side.

Tracey stands next to me and looks at my saucer. 'Can I have some?'

'No!' says Mom. 'Not unless you've bitten your tongue off as well. Have you? No? Didn't think so.'

Dad looks at Tracey. 'What you both was doing?'

'We were just playing, Dad, and then Mandy went on the table to sing "I can't get no satisfaction."'

Dad throws back his head and brays like a horse. He can hardly talk for laughing. 'You get some satisfaction now, ain't it, Mandy?'

Mom tries hard not to laugh with him, I can see her eyes crease at the side, but then she watches me sliding the ice cream around the stitches on my swollen tongue and tells me to go and lie down. It takes ages for the swelling to go down and I get special ice-cream breakfasts and ice-cream dinners for weeks while I lisp and splutter.

One day, I'm in the garden playing with Karen in the pram.

'Give me a kith,' I say to her and when the others hear they start to copy me, chasing me around the garden with a sing-song chant.

'Kit, kit, kit,' they say and add it to the list of my names: Skins, Patches, Minty, Kit.

8

Oh, Island in the Sun

Sometimes, Dad comes home with packages and carries them like precious things into the kitchen. He opens them carefully and draws out lengths of navy-blue mohair or black worsted wool. Suit lengths, he calls them.

'Back home I could get somebody make me a good three-piece suit with this. Beautiful.'

He buys gauzy cotton shirts pinned on cardboard, embroidered handkerchiefs with matching ties laid together in satin-lined boxes, and socks so fine you can see straight through them. And shoes. Shoes galore.

'Look this,' he says quietly.

There are two boxes. He opens the first and cradles a new pair of shoes in his hand like he did with my little sister when she was first born.

'You see the sole?' he says in awe. 'Leather. You must be careful. A man could slip on this.'

Then he turns it over. 'Moccasin. I just see them and buy them. Beautiful.'

He rewraps the shoe in its paper and nestles it next to its twin.

'Look,' he says again, carefully lifting the lid of the next box like there might be a kitten inside or a poisonous snake. 'Chelsea boots.'

He turns them and stares, holds them up to the light. Puts them sole first on the table and nudges them round with the tip of his finger, beauty queens on the podium. 'What a pissing good shoe.'

My mother says nothing. She is washing up, she is ironing, she is mopping the floor.

Eventually, when the worship of the shoes is over, he takes both boxes upstairs and leaves us to roam the house in search of old bread and economy margarine.

Uncle Mike is just the opposite. He looks so much like my dad they could be brothers, but where Dad is sour, he is sweet; where my father is mean, Uncle Mike has his arms wide open. He's my dad's cousin, a big brown bear of a man. Loud, gruff, rough, fun, always talking, joking, wobbling into the house with his big teeth bared. No Chelsea boots for Uncle Mike, no Italian leather moccasins with a slippery sole. Uncle Mike's shoes are old, broken down at the back, big lace-up boots that he doesn't polish. In the summer, big, battered, leather sandals hang off his dusty feet with the yellow nails. Uncle Mike doesn't shave and nothing on him matches, not even his socks. He is perfect in every way.

It's always without warning, completely out of the blue. Uncle Mike throws open the front door with no knock and walks in, laughing.

'Heh, heh! Where you all is?'

We hear his voice and run from all over the house and jump on him. Dean hangs off his arm and I get a finger or a thumb.

'Lord God! Dean, you getting big, eh?' covering the whole of my brother's head with his palm. 'Mandy, Mandy! Come, Tracey! Come, Kim! Yes. Come!'

'Where The Rock?' he asks Mom.

'Cricket,' she says. Hard voice, hint of menace. There is no hello, there is no cup of tea. She doesn't like Uncle Mike and his scruffy, bachelor ways, she doesn't like his spontaneous visits and loud voice, his rickety van and the love he gets from us. She will never let go of the things he used to say about white women, how he wanted Dad to wait for the woman he left behind in St Kitts. She lets things out from time to time and we have to piece it all together, the months she spent living with my father in one room while Mike and the other Kittians partied in the rest of the house. Then there were wives and girlfriends, the black women who turned their noses up at the slack white pieces who couldn't clean and couldn't cook, who went with any black man they could get their hands on, who got pregnant in five minutes before they could even get married. When they were all together, they'd be telling stories in their West Indian accents, stories about home and laughs and sunshine and rum and cricket and card games, dances and jokes she'll never understand. Mom wants all of my father, not the bit of him on offer – she wants his past as well.

But Uncle Mike has come for us and we know it. We don't have to get ready in our meeting clothes, we don't have to have our hair plaited or our faces wiped. He'll take us just as we come. He picks up Karen and balances her on his big belly and whisks the rest of us out of the house and into his campervan. 'St Christopher Steel Band' it says on the side with a flag of St Kitts and the island's coat of arms badly painted and slightly on the lean. We scramble around for a seat among the pans and sticks, the drum stands, blankets and old clothes.

We don't have to behave and sit still with Uncle Mike. We don't have to watch what we say or what we wear, we can hug him and touch him and feel his rough white bristles, hold his huge brown hands, touch his things, pull levers, laugh, mess about. We lurch from seat to seat as he dashes the clattering van round corners with the radio on, his belly hard against the steering wheel, busting out his deep baritone and singing, all of us together, '*Oh, island in the sun . . .*'

We pull up outside a rough-looking house and Mike bounces the campervan off the street into the front yard. This is the same house my mother and father used to share with him, the place where I was born, Wordsworth Road in Small Heath, where my father's friends – Grumble, Rudy, Uncle Mike and the other members of the steel band – still live, those men who didn't meet a white woman and move to the white areas, to the respectable side of town.

Mike pulls open the door and we dash out into his small, haphazard bedsit on the ground floor at the back of the house. There's a vast iron bedstead with messy blankets and pillows, there's a threadbare rug and an old black-and-white telly propped up on bricks in one corner. A curtain separates his bedroom from the kitchen. There's never a woman around, we have him all to ourselves.

He always thinks ahead. We are always hungry. There's a pyramid of Johnny Cakes waiting for us, crispy and golden, and a pan of steaming saltfish that he doles out on saucers and plates. Dean gets his share in a big mug.

I break my Johnny Cake in half and dip the warm, fluffy insides into the slick of yellow oil and gobble it down. I'm lost in the taste. There's more and there's more and there's more. All we can eat.

The kitchenette is tiny, hardly big enough for a scratched wooden table, a two-ring hob and white stone sink.

'Come! Come!' he says, clapping his hands. 'Carrot juice!'

He tips enormous carrots out of a paper bag and starts chivvying us.

'Look, grate them up. Careful you fingers! Take time, take time! You don't like it, is it, Mandy? No wonder you so meagre. Add the condense milk, little, little. Now the nutmeg. Easy!'

There is a big belly laugh between every sentence, everything is a joke, everything is OK, nothing is wrong. We make a mess and eventually we make the carrot juice.

When it's made, we sit cross-legged on the floor or the bed and Uncle Mike laughs and talks about back home.

'So, The Rock playing cricket? Lord God, he love to play. You know why we call him The Rock?'

Dean puts his hand up like we're at school. 'He's big.'

'He big, yes, but it was because when you stand him by the wicket, you couldn't get him out. A six and a four and a six and four and sometimes a two, you couldn't bowl him! The whole island know about Arthur O'Loughlin. He was Arthur Louard then, he had his mother's name. He was the best cricketer in the whole of St Kitts, the whole of the islands.'

'Did you play cricket, Uncle Mike?' I ask.

'Me?' He jiggles his belly. 'Me and this?' He laughs, throws his head back and show us his big yellow teeth. Then he lights a cigarette.

'When O'Loughlin hear about the boy playing cricket so good, he tell everyone that The Rock is his son. Claim him. He didn't say nothing before but now he was somebody. And O'Loughlin was proud, he was my uncle too. Proud, proud man. We was all proud of Arthur O'Loughlin.'

He makes a half-hearted attempt to tidy up the mess we've made. We gather up our things and stack them as best we can on the draining board. He's still talking.

'You know what else they call him, you father? Lofty, because he is tall, even taller than me. And Kid Mirror. Man couldn't stop look at himself. Good-looking, you see. Not like you Uncle Mike.'

When we get home, Dad's in the kitchen in his cricket whites, his big kitbag on the floor.

'Lofty!' says Uncle Mike. 'You win?'

We catch the odd word between them, wickets, overs, seams and who bowled who, and my dad throwing his arm up in the air with the invisible ball.

'Bam!' he says, 'LBW!' and Mike laughing and laughing until he looks over at my mother.

She doesn't leave the room. She doesn't join in. She stands and listens with her arms folded, waiting for him to leave. She'll have to listen to our stories later, Uncle Mike did this and Uncle Mike said that and we had this to eat and that to eat and how great he is, how great. She'll purse her lips and tell us counter stories of his womanizing and drinking, a grown man still living in the same room he had since the boat landed, playing cards and music when he could have made something of himself.

There's a silence suddenly and Uncle Mike claps his hands.

'Me gone,' he says suddenly. We stand in the street and wave and wave until he's out of sight.

9

A Brand-new Brother

It's Thursday night and we've been to the meeting. Conrad came with us. Conrad is coming to our house more and more, and doing things like taking us to the park and staying overnight. He's two years older than Kim and taller than everyone except Dad. He used to have a stutter but he's got over it now. He used to have a West Indian accent but that has gone as well.

We pile into the kitchen, hungry after the long walk home from the bus stop. We had to get off early because we didn't have enough money to stay on the bus that takes us right up Springfield Road. As soon as we're through the door, we start looking for something to eat. There's nothing there, no bread, no cream crackers, no margarine, either. Kim says she'll make some porridge.

'Remember Black Nana's porridge?' I say. 'Remember the lumps? It was disgusting.'

'Yeah, she used to make porridge for me as well when we lived in the West Indies,' says Conrad.

'Who did?' I ask.

'Nana. Chrissie.'

'You mean Black Nana?'

'Yeah.'

We stop what we are doing and look at him. He doesn't speak much and when he does it's not usually to tell us things he can't possibly know.

'How do you know Black Nana?' I ask.

He frowns and looks from one face to another. 'She's my granny as well.'

There's nothing for a while. Not a sound. Then the questions start, all of us piling in, crowding round him, and when he tells us that he's our brother, that he came to England from St Kitts when he was six, that his mom and my dad are his parents and that they had him in the West Indies before any of us were born, that he's as scared of Dad as we are, we all start laughing. It's one of the most exciting days of my life, of all of our lives. Of course he's my brother, I always knew, I never knew. I look at him and look at him and see my dad in his eyes, in his height, in his hands. I see Dean in him, and if I see the others in him, then I see myself. He's part of me and I am part of him and I am so excited I can't stop talking.

'Why didn't you tell us?' I ask.

'I thought you knew,' he says. 'I thought Dad told you, or Sheila.' But they told us nothing. Never. He was one of the children who Mom looked after, he was a boy from school. They never said we had a brother. And then he tells us about Black Nana, his nana.

'She loved me, spoiled me rotten. I can see her now. Every time she looked at me she used to smile. Me and my mother used to visit her and she'd cook great big dinners for us. She was great.'

Was she? Was she ever great? Was she great when she was back home on her own porch, shading from the boiling sun under a blue, blue sky by the blue, blue sea? I imagine Black Nana without her bandana, with the wavy hair she had when she left us, shuffling unsteadily down the hallway. I see her holding Conrad's hand maybe, smiling maybe, waving her son off to England and then waiting. All the time thinking, 'Any day now, Arthur will send for Conrad and send for his girlfriend, Catherine, and they can be a family again.' And maybe she was thinking there would be more Conrads and girl Conrads who she could sit and kiss and ply with treats like she did with Tracey. And maybe they would make a home for her with them and they could all be a family together.

But five years later when Dad sends home for someone to come to England, it's for her, not for Catherine, not for Conrad. And he's only asking because he wants help. He wants her to come over and look after some white woman's house under grey, grey skies so far from the sea you couldn't get any further if you tried. Yes, come over and look after some white woman's half-black children, miserable and thin, who look just like their mother and don't want Black Nana around. Only Tracey managed to get through her armour.

And I think of Conrad's mother, the quiet, pretty black woman who used to come and collect Conrad from our house. That woman is my dad's ex-girlfriend, the one he left behind with a one-year-old baby, who has to come calling round to our house and thank my mother for looking after her son while she goes to work. That must be the deal. Dad has to look after his son while Catherine goes to work. And I feel sorry for them all, Mom and Dad and Catherine and Chrissie and the mess they all made, and

Dean and Karen and Kim and Tracey and me myself for not knowing my brother for so many years.

We cluster around Conrad, our brand-new brother, for the rest of the night, asking him questions about who is who and when and how and what the West Indies was like and who his other brother is and who his other sister is and the new man who married his mom and now he has two dads and what's that like and where he lives and what he thinks, and the questions go on and on for ages, and when he goes home we feel bigger somehow, better, more complete with him in our lives.

He comes and goes. He is part of us. He comes in without knocking. He eats what we eat if there's food, he eats nothing if there's nothing there. He gets older and more handsome. He gets tough and manly and as big as my dad. He visits with beautiful girls who hang on his every word. I try to copy how they sit and walk, and covet their long leather coats and centre partings. He talks about football with Dad and takes Dean to the Blues.

My mom loves him. He calls her 'Sheila' in his quiet way, shy and respectful to a fault. We watch *Carry On* films on a Saturday when Dad is out and laugh together, learning the lines, repeating them.

He is always in our hearts.

10

Fish and Chips

'Fish and chips!' Mom bellows up the stairs. Excited voice. Without warning.

There are two fish-and-chip shops. The best one and the nearest one. The best one is down College Road, opposite the public toilets by the skinny River Cole that dribbles under Stratford Road on its way to better places.

We hardly ever have fish and chips; sometimes, on rare days, out of the blue, she'll buy us a bag of chips to share, a single bag between the five of us. Only Mom has fish. She always comes back breathless from running home with the big parcel wrapped in newspaper. She places it like a newborn on the kitchen table and rips the paper into five squares. We gather round and watch as she portions the chips out evenly, five shares for us and a smaller cluster for herself. Sometimes she buys a bottle of red sauce that she wallops on its bottom until it splodges all over our food.

I try to make my share last, to eat carefully with two delicate fingers like I have meals banked up ahead of me and all the time in the world. I want to gobble it down, all in one, lick the paper, ball it up in my fist and throw it over my shoulder. I want to run away with my chips in my paper square and wallow in the smell and the feel of hot food in my belly and salt on my fingers. I eat standing up, like the others. I eat gratefully, quickly, and it's gone in minutes. But Mom's hasn't.

The fish is still there on the paper, glistening in oil, steaming, massive. We watch her like gargoyles. She only cooks for Dad but never eats with him. She picks at food, she snacks and breaks bread into pieces and eats a bit of it, a crust, a tear. But every so often she forgets she doesn't like to eat and is consumed by the occasion, her whole being given over to a pie, a cake, a piece of fish.

Her hand moves from food to mouth, from food to mouth, over and over. First, she peels the golden batter, so soaked in vinegar that it stings our noses. She folds it into her mouth, loads it in, eats it with her eyes closed. She eats with deliberation, nudging the bright-white flesh until it comes away in warm, slippery chunks. She makes noises at the base of her throat that make us jealous. We cluster around her and, when she's had enough of our silent beseeching, she pops a bit in our open mouths and tells us to go away.

That Friday night after she bellows up the stairs, she goes to the fish-and-chip shop and comes back with Lorraine.

We are hungry and we are waiting. We prowl the kitchen, ready to pounce on her return. There's bread for butties and margarine and a rogue jar of pickled onions that we hold to the light and count.

'There's only four,' says Kim. 'Mom will have one and we'll share the others.'

'Cut them now,' I say.

'No, we'll wait.' Kim's the oldest and she's eleven. She can say things like that.

'Where is she?' I ask no one, everyone.

'Bet she's talking to someone,' says Kim. 'Go and see if she's coming.'

But she's nowhere on our street. I trot to the corner, but she's not walking up Passey Road with our chips under her arm, she's not laughing with Marge, saying their goodbyes. We have to take it in turns to wait by the gate until it gets too cold, too dark. Dad's watching the telly, but there's no point in telling him we're hungry or that his wife's gone missing with a promise. He's not bothered about how long she takes because he's had his dinner. We haven't.

Eventually, we give up. This has happened before. She's left the house and started talking to some woman she knows on Stratford Road before she's even got to the chip shop and she's come home with nothing. Or she's talking to a stranger in the chip shop while our chips are frying in the oil and she's letting people go ahead of her in the queue. She's doing something else, somewhere else, without thinking about us, and we won't be eating before midnight, if at all. We take our empty bellies and push open the door to the telly room. We slink in silently and sink into the sofa to fill up on John Wayne or Audie Murphy, to watch whatever Dad is watching, a detective show, a black-and-white film, the news.

His eyes swivel towards us for a moment, which means 'Do not make a sound,' but then the front door opens and we tumble over one another, hunger winning out over Dad's wrath, to get to the door and dash out to the hall. Mom is there in the porch and a girl is with her.

'Go on through,' Mom says to the girl and points her down the hallway towards the kitchen.

The girl is older than us, with long hair and freckles. She is crying and her two front teeth are crooked. I can't stop looking at her teeth and the way they bite down on her lip. I don't understand how she can look pretty and ugly at the same time. She's wearing a massive tartan coat and, as she walks past us, she pulls it hard across her body. Mom follows behind. The chips are nowhere to be seen.

'Go and watch the telly,' she hisses and shoos us away. She closes the door to the kitchen and that's that. We can't even get to the bread and pickled onions. Dad barely turns his head when we slink back in, starving, and find somewhere to sit, but we know he has registered the disturbance and if there is any more noise or fuss or 'if you all can't keep quiet . . .' we will be banished. So we don't tell him about the weeping girl who ate our chips. I snuggle in between Kim and Tracey; their warmth will have to fill me up.

In the morning, she's still in our house, the girl with the crooked teeth. She's sitting in the kitchen with Mom but smiling now, wearing a red plastic clip in her hair. She's got an empty plate in front of her so she's probably had toast, which probably means there's no bread left. I hurry to the packet and quickly spread margarine on the last two pieces, fold them in half and gobble them down. Mom and the girl have a mug of tea each, both of them holding it like a precious thing, two hands around the bowl.

'This. Is. Lorraine,' Mom says as I chew. She's speaking to me with her 'I am talking to an idiot' voice on and it's for Lorraine's benefit to show her how she helps her children learn things by speaking very slowly in a very Brummie accent.

'Hello,' I say and smile with the bread stuck in the gap between my teeth. I cover my mouth with my hand and try to suck it out.

'This is Mandy. Number two.'

Lorraine holds out her hand like I'm a grown-up. It's warm from the tea and soft and I worry that when the others come down I'll have to share her with numbers one and three. Dean won't count because he's a boy and neither will Karen because she won't understand how pretty Lorraine is and how she's going to make me her best friend.

'Don't stare,' says Mom. 'Tell the others to get up. There's jobs to be done.'

When I go back to tell Tracey about the girl, I realize that Dean has been sleeping in our room on the floor.

'Mom said get up.' I throw the blankets off Dean, who, still in his sleep, pulls them back over himself. Kim is asleep and that's so normal I don't even try to rouse her. She stays up all night reading and then she can't wake up in the morning. We usually leave her to it.

I sit on our bed and whisper to Tracey.

'That girl's downstairs.'

'From yesterday?'

'Lorraine, that's her name.'

Tracey is scratching her eczema. 'Why?' she says.

'I don't know. She's really pretty.'

'I know. I saw her.'

'She's eaten all the bread,' I lie. I can't be blamed.

Me and Tracey go downstairs to the kitchen to look at the girl and try to understand why she's sleeping in Dean's room. To get the most information you have to look like you don't want it. Everyone knows that. We wander around the room, looking for food, putting on the kettle for sweet tea, pretending to play with things.

Mom's found a new way of speaking for Lorraine; it's a lofty strain of 'idiot' voice called 'imparting knowledge'.

'. . . yes, all five of them in nine years. I don't recommend it, Lorraine. Hard work it is. I always wanted children, the more the better, but they're expensive. And Arthur wants to go home. Saves every penny. So we're a bit pinched here. But you're welcome, love. Welcome as anyone could be. I know what it's like to be thrown out for love.' She sniffs as an invitation to Lorraine to ask her to continue.

But Lorraine is slow and Mom has to continue without the prompt.

'After we fell in love . . .'

Tracey side-eyes me.

'After we fell in love, me and Arthur, my mother threw me out. I'm Irish, you see. She came here for a better life, she said. And she didn't want a daughter who went with a black man. So I had to move in with Arthur. One room in a shared house. Kim was born there.'

'Are you Kim?' Lorraine says to Tracey.

Mom laughs. 'This is number three. Kim's number one.' She reaches over and shoves Tracey towards the door. 'Go and tell her to get up. It's nearly ten o'clock.' Then she's off again, wafting in a pink haze down memory lane, down Stratford Road, veering off to Small Heath and number 32 Wordsworth Road where it all started.

*

That night we're all in the telly room watching *The Man in the Suitcase*. Dad is in his chair and Mom sits on the floor in front, leaning against his legs.

'Where's the girl?' he asks.

Mom turns round. Caring voice. 'Dean's room. She's six months gone.'

'Hmmm,' he says.

'What could I do, Arthur? She was just sitting there on that bench by the traffic lights, sobbing her heart out. Said she had nowhere to go. Her mom had thrown her out. I know what that feels like. It took me right back. I couldn't leave her there, could I?'

'Where she come from?'

'Solihull, I think. She said she'd been walking for hours. Couldn't go any further.'

Dad says nothing for ages. We are barely breathing in case we miss some of the story.

'Where's the boy?' he says after a while, his eyes on the screen. *Man in the Suitcase* is coming to the climax of the episode where, through his cunning and superior knowledge of international travel, he has solved the case, he has the baddies in front of him. He has a gun. They don't. He's telling them how they did it, they were clever, yes, but they made one fatal mistake. We are torn between which story to follow.

'She didn't say. I think he's left her.'

Dad absorbs the end of *Man in the Suitcase*, where the baddies are finally arrested by the police and led away, scowling. When the adverts start, he looks down at his wife.

'Dean's a boy. A boy needs his own room.'

'I know, Arthur,' she says quietly. 'But you make mistakes for love, don't you? She's a good girl who's got into trouble. What else could I do?'

That summer Lorraine is everywhere. Helping with the housework, playing with Karen and Dean, tidying the kitchen, sweeping the path, washing, ironing, smiling at Dad and somehow keeping completely out of his way. She plays with us at the top of the garden, she colours in with us at the kitchen table, she reads us stories at bedtime, and all the while her belly gets bigger and bigger.

She tucks me and Kim in one night and sees me looking at the massive bulge in front of her. I can't believe there is a curled-up baby in there.

'He'll be out soon. You can hold him if you like,' she says. She's always smiling these days, her two beautiful, crooked teeth long and white and perfect. 'I'm not looking forward to the birth but your mom says it's not as bad as people say and she's had five so she must know what she's talking about.'

'I don't want to have babies,' I say. 'I don't want them to unravel me.'

'What?'

'I don't want them to undo the knot and unravel me.'

Lorraine looks at me for a long time.

'Do you know how babies come out?' she says.

'Yes. Through your belly button. They undo the knot and unravel your skin, then tie it up again. I saw it on a programme.'

Lorraine is smiling when she pulls the blankets up

around my neck. Kim is reading her book and not interested in Lorraine and conversations about babies. Tracey is asleep.

'Babies come out between your legs,' she says. 'Not out of your bum, either. And definitely not out of your belly button.'

She kisses my forehead and pats the blanket. 'Night night.'

When she's gone, I think about last year when my mom was pregnant with Karen. She kept sitting down all the time because she was tired and she kept saying the baby was heavy. I remember the weight of it when Mom gave me a hold of her straight after she was born.

The size of that baby was massive and it would be literally impossible for it to come out of the tiny hole where the wee comes out. Lorraine hasn't got any other babies, not like my mom, who has now had five. I feel sorry for Lorraine when she switches off the light and goes back to Dean's bedroom. Someone should tell her the truth.

One day, when I'm coming up the road from school, I see Lorraine standing by the front door. She's a bit red in the face.

'Hello, love,' she says, but she looks straight past me, craning her neck up and down the street, her hands holding one another over and over. I walk into the kitchen and Mom shakes her head.

'She'll make herself ill.'

Suddenly there's a commotion and Lorraine hurries down the hallway, one hand on her belly. 'I can see him!' she cries.

KIT DE WAAL

I dash back to the front gate where she now stands smoothing her dress over her belly, her face fully alive and her lovely smile broad and trembling. She's waving at a man in full sailor uniform, a navy hat on the back of his head, a white bib over his shoulders. He's got a giant rucksack and a tight, rolling walk.

'Dougie!' she shouts and starts to wave. He waves back and nods as if to say, 'I see you!'

Then she's out of the gate and waddling down Springfield Road and he's caught her round the shoulders and kissing her for all the neighbours to see. Mom is standing at the front door with a tea towel in her hand and tears in her eyes.

'Ah!' she says. 'Look at that.'

He shakes Mom's hand. 'Dougie,' he says.

Tracey and me nudge each other because of his outfit and the smell of beer and because he's Scottish and because we know this is a big moment in Lorraine's life and because Mom looks a bit flustered by his handsome face.

'Come in, come in, come in,' she says.

They walk hand in hand, past me and Tracey at the gate, into the front room where nobody ever goes, and Mom shushes me into the kitchen, flapping the tea towel like I'm a fly at a picnic.

'Who is he?' I ask.

'He's the mistake she made, love. He's heartache.'

'Shall I take them in a cup of tea?'

But Mom doesn't answer. She props her head on her hand and stares out of the window with glassy eyes.

84

Dougie takes Lorraine away after she has their baby boy. He gets them a flat somewhere far away and I have to imagine what the baby will look like when he grows up and if his teeth will fold over at the front like Lorraine's.

One day, a letter comes and Mom reads it up by the front door.

'Oh, Lorraine,' she says and starts to cry. Dad asks her what's wrong and she sniffs her way through the wedding and Lorraine making it up with her mother and the baby boy dressed as a page and Lorraine saying thank you for everything, and then she stops suddenly.

'I'm an idiot. She never even invited me.' She folds the letter up, puts it in the pocket of her apron and pushes past Dad on her way to hang out the washing.

He shakes his head and says the usual. 'You mother is a crazy woman.'

11

God and Four Women

There's an interesting side to Stratford Road and a boring side. One side has shops that sell sweets, clothes, shoes, cakes, Woolworths, chips and Ace Value, which spills mop buckets and garden rakes on to the pavement. The other side has the barber's, the garage, the travel agent and the launderette.

The barber is Mario, a squat Italian with navy-black hair and a tight, high bum. He sculpts his beard into perfect, elaborate shapes that give him the illusion of a neck and cheekbones. He wears tight bell-bottom trousers with a thick black belt, his T-shirt tucked in. When he's not cutting hair, he struts about the pavement with a neat little broom he wields like a majorette, which, as far as I can tell, never makes contact with the ground. Sometimes he leans on the door of his shop underneath the slowly spinning red-and-white sign. I see Mario every day because his shop is right by the bus stop and he always watches me waiting. There's something troubling about Mario. I feel like he wants to speak to me or eat me and I can't decide if he's good or bad.

After Lorraine leaves, Mom gets a new job. She's has lots of jobs to do in the house and cleaning other people's houses too but now she also cleans the new mini-market on Stratford Road every afternoon after she collects Karen and Dean from school. It's only been open for a few weeks, a really big shop like you see on American films where people can walk down the aisles and choose their own food and put it in a plastic basket. Not like Kent's, where you had to wait and see what tin Mrs Kent selected for you. There are packets of food you've never seen before, different brands of margarine and beans, tins of fruit, Mr Kipling cakes and frozen food in three massive freezers.

Mom wears a special chocolate-coloured overall for her job that has 'MacFisheries' embroidered on the back and the front in glowing yellow cotton. For weeks and weeks, it's 'MacFisheries' this and 'MacFisheries' that.

She comes home with dented tins and opened packets that she's got at a reduced rate and puts them in the pantry where we can't touch them without getting into trouble.

'Oh, we do a special coffee at MacFisheries. They don't do it anywhere else. People come from Solihull to buy it. Solihull.'

She has a MacFisheries plastic bag that she folds in half carefully and then folds again and puts in her shopping trolley.

'At MacFisheries there are three separate tills. You can go through any one you like. I'd love to be on the tills but you have to be specially trained.'

She takes off her apron and folds it in half and then half again.

'When I'd finished mopping, Graham, that's the manager – he's only about twenty-five – asked me if I'd clean the windows as well because of the rain.'

'Specially,' Tracey says under her breath.

But Mom never gets promoted to the till. She never gets

trained or catches the eye of the infant Graham. She just tidies up the shelves and cleans the floor with a special MacFisheries mop.

Between five o'clock and six o'clock every night she's completely idle for one whole hour, which adds up to seven hours every week when she's not earning, and she tells us it's important she keeps bringing the money in. So she finds something to do with her leisure time and that's cleaning the launderette. We never mind about going to the Laundrama to help Mom. For a start, it's always warm inside. Even on a summer's day, I love how the warmth seeps into my skin and muscles, into my bones and my shoulders. The Laundrama smells of clean, of freshness, of things being put right, of order and properness.

We would never take our washing to the Laundrama. It costs too much money. We do our washing in the wash house at the back of our house between the kitchen and the garden. Grey-green glass hangs uncertainly overhead, resting between rotting wooden struts. Rain always leaks through on to the concrete floor, permanently damp and uneven, pitted and cracked. Off the wash house is an old toilet behind a rough plank door. There's no light. If you dare to go to that toilet, you have to leave the door open a little bit otherwise demons and ghosts will eat you, spiders will fall into your hair and burrow their way into your brain and lay their eggs there.

Wash day is a hot, wet, messy, awkward palaver. You have to position the twin-tub washing machine in the middle of the wash house so you can plug it in through the kitchen window. It's big and rusty on the side with two lids, one for the washer and one for the spinner. You have to gather the washing from all over the house and put it in different piles. Once the machine's going, you have to push the clothes down in the warm water as a big central arm gyrates and sloshes the clothes around. We've got a massive pair of wooden tongs for putting the clothes in and getting them out. You can fish things out early if they're not very dirty and put them into the other smaller tub that's for spinning the water out of the laundry, where, if you're not careful, you can break your wrist by trying to catch the clothes before the cycle has stopped.

Sometimes the mangle is enlisted for extra drying power. It's also rusty and heavy and awkward and liable to break or squash some bit of you if you're not paying attention.

When the washing is still damp, Mom always makes us carry it with us to the Laundrama in big carrier bags to be dried. Massive washing machines line one side of the long room and on the other side there are three big rollers for ironing and five huge tumble dryers in lemon yellow. Two wall-mounted machines sell soap powder by the plastic cupful and another sells soda crystals, which look like sweets but taste like acid. Yet another machine sells blue plastic laundry bags and right at the back is the office where Mom keeps her cleaning stuff.

As soon as we walk in, one of us flips the sign from 'Open' to 'Closed' and the game starts, the hunt for lost coins. They are mostly under the dryers, a sixpence or thruppence that someone dropped or couldn't reach.

What we find, we keep. It's the best game ever. Dean always levers himself down behind the machines and the rollers because he's the size of a big pixie. That's where the most coins roll so he always ends up with the most money.

We each get a cloth and start wiping the excess powder from the little bays in the washers and clean out the dust from the dryers. We have to collect the laundry baskets from wherever they are and pick up dropped socks and buttons and put them all in the office.

While she's cleaning and mopping, Mom pops our clothes in the warmest dryer and gets one of us to find her a lost coin to make it start. I always get the job of opening the door really quickly and taking out the driest things and quickly slamming the door shut before the drum has stopped spinning. I'm a bit of an expert. I like to fold the clothes when they are still warm and smooth out the last few creases. I pile them up in size order, in colour order, and once they are cool, I place them carefully back in the bag.

Mom always brings sheets and pillowcases for the two giant industrial ironing rollers just inside the front door. You have to turn them on and then two of you have to hold the very edge of the sheet and slowly feed it between the white, cushioned, turning rollers. The sheet goes in one side and comes out at the top of the other, flat, soft, warm and perfect. You have to be really careful not to put your hand in as you ease the edge of the sheet in because once someone did that and their hand was ironed down to paper thickness like something off *Tom and Jerry*. That's what Mom said and it's not hard to believe.

Sometimes when we get there, other women are just finishing up and because Mom knows everyone, she spends half her time saying hello and gossiping. If I keep myself busy with little jobs, they don't notice that I'm listening. There's a sort of party atmosphere, the folding and unfolding of arms, nudges, whispered things about men and hussies, who's been eating hot bread and is already showing, who's borrowing money and can't pay, who told what to whom and got a slap for it or a kiss or a win on the Pools or Spot the Ball. Or a divorce. Divorce makes every woman stop and stare. It's the ultimate disgrace.

'Didn't I say?' says Hilda from Grove Road. 'Didn't I say there was something wrong in that house?'

'She should give him a taste of his own medicine, see how he fares without her for a few weeks,' says Betty With the Eye. 'That'd bring him to heel.'

'Few weeks, yes,' mutters Peggy Devlin. 'You wouldn't take it as far as the divorce courts.'

'No need,' says one. 'Never,' says another. 'He'd have learned his lesson,' says the third. And my mother can't help it.

'Divorce is only allowed in the case of adultery. That's what the Bible says.'

They say nothing. One gives a sniff of assent. Who can stand against God and four women in a launderette?

'Give us a song, Dean, love,' says Hilda by way of a full stop.

'Go on!' says Betty.

He clambers up on to the big dryers and stands there with his hands on his hips, his knees white with unoiled summer skin. His hair curls up at all angles, his arms are skinny, snappable. He's wearing red summer sandals that he's outgrown and Mom has done her usual trick of taking a Stanley knife to the front, cutting away an inch of leather so his toes can peek out. He has to buckle them on extra tight to make them stay on. Once in a while, without warning and for no reason we can fathom, Mom makes him wear a pair of green leather lederhosen for the day. She found them in a jumble sale and said they were a special bargain all the way from Germany, and they'd last forever, but they are too hot for the summer so he's wearing normal shorts made out of trousers that had a hole in the knee. His smile is wide and confident.

'"It's Not Unusual"!' I shout and he nods like a Las Vegas crooner being handed the mic. He opens his arms wide and starts. He knows all the words, all the moves. The women are clapping and laughing and shaking their heads.

'Oooh, he's so good!'

'Little heartbreaker, he is.'

'You'll have to keep your eye on this one, Sheila.'

Even we, who have seen his routines dozens of times, have to stop and watch. He hops over the gaps between the machines in his dangerous red sandals, slipping on the metal. He struts to the end of the run and sashays back, working his way through the song, working his way through the women, right to the last note, but there's barely a beat before he segues seamlessly into Johnny Cash, Gene Pitney, Adam Faith.

We all watch, old women and young. Mom stops her

jobs and we all gather round, looking up at the boy child as he prances and dances, every intonation, word perfect, until, at the end of our concert, when the audience has gone home, he has sixpences and sweets and a bellyful of adoration. We walk home warm and happy, our jobs done, sucking a sticky sweet from Dean's massive haul.

Every morning, Mom puts the radio on loud. We wake up and shuffle downstairs to a cold kitchen and *Housewives' Choice* with slick Jimmy Young. He plays songs from the hit parade – Val Doonican, Gene Pitney, Sandy Shaw – and Mom sings along.

'I love this,' she says and turns the dial. 'Frank Ifield.

It's not long before she has forgotten to put margarine on the bread or make the tea and she clasps a tea towel to her chest and throws her head back, adding the obligatory yodel. She sings every single word of every single verse and we know there will be no bringing her back to Springfield Road until the song is done. And even then.

We get up and make our own breakfast while she stands in the middle of the kitchen, her eyes closed, until Jimmy tells us that it's half past eight and she comes to. She looks around the kitchen like she's never seen it before. She's been far, far away.

'Hurry up,' she mutters. 'You'll be late.'

12

Sandwiches

We're waiting for Mom outside the Irish shop on Stratford Road. She's buying the things we will eat at Nan's, who can't be expected to put up with a whole tribe of us being hungry as well as poor as well as half black. So Mom always brings a shopping bag of stuff that she places on Nan's clean, bright-red kitchen table, one by one, the squash, the bread, the margarine, the ham, the cheese triangles, the biscuits.

Margaret Doyle, or Nan, is an altogether different woman to my father's mother. A farmer's daughter from Wexford, she's sharp and small like a dangerous tack. Old photographs show a firm, dark-eyed woman with short black hair and a Spanish look, but by the time we come to know her she is grey and worn down from her hard life as the mother of nine and landlady to dozens.

Nan is as neat as a pin, like the tall Edwardian house she shares with Grandad in the Irish part of town, the many rooms tidy and empty now her children are gone. Nan wears pastel twinsets and smooth woollen skirts in lavender and grey, with support stockings of an intense tan and soft leather shoes, misshapen where her bunions press and stretch the sides. Her hair is set every week and sprayed into a stiff grey aura and her ivory dentures are always sparkly and clean. She's as tiny as my mother with a quickness about her, a throaty laugh and a vinegar tongue.

She seems to be always organizing my grandfather Nicholas.

'In the kitchen with you now, Nick.'

'You're to sit here, Dad. This chair. Sit yourself down.'

'You'll want some tea, Nick.'

Nick is slow and quiet, his red hair cropped short, Depression-style. His accent is thick and country, whispery and light; there's nothing loud about him. She dresses him in check shirts with V-neck jumpers and well-ironed trousers. His shoes are good, stout leather and polished to perfection. The two of them are a credit to themselves, that's how she puts it, and that is important to her.

Whenever we visit, Nan has to have us employed. We know we are not in the same league as our white cousins, the children of Greta, of Michael, of Jimmy, Kevin or Mary, who have had the Catholic decency, at least, to marry of their own kind. We hardly see them. They must visit on other days when we're not expected, not wanted.

Nan always finds something for our brown fingers to do that's useful, endless and silent. Her favourite thing is the button box, a big, embroidered felt box for cotton and thread, needles, elastic and hundreds of buttons. We love it. She makes us sit on the floor and we have to tidy it, wind the threads neatly on themselves and put the needles on card in size order, tuck the elastic against the side of the box so it won't unravel, stack the thimbles, pick out the fluff and dust. And when we finish, we stack the buttons, big to small, into little piles that we call 'cakes', using a pearl or a black bead for the top. She must mess it up especially before we come so we have something to do because it's always untidy, the ribbons and bias binding intertwined and knotted.

As soon as the button box comes out, Grandad reaches for his accordion, puts the leather strap over his shoulder and rests the box on his knee like a baby.

'We'll have a song now,' he says.

The first pull is discordant and breathy. He eases it into something beautiful, 'The Wild Colonial Boy', 'The Patriot Game' or 'I'll Take You Home Again, Kathleen', songs we have heard from him all our lives. We sing with him as his long labourer's fingers dance over the keys, jerking and folding the box, jerking and folding as it breathes and hums, his feet tapping the beat, his head inclined to the light. It's peaceful and easy with Grandad, who only speaks through his music, song after song, until we're called into the kitchen to eat the sandwiches and have a biscuit each, an iced ring or a Rich Tea. We have watery orange squash and have to wash our hands afterwards. On rare days, Nan's made an apple pie, but because she makes it with honey instead of sugar it's not sweet enough for me and I am suspicious of her generosity.

Sometimes, on the way home, Mom tells us about the father she knew, the young Nick, and puts a different complexion on things. She weaves a tale of a farmhand and a farmer's daughter all the way from the fields of Campile, across the water to a flat above a shop in the Irish quarter of Birmingham. He was working the building sites then.

'He used to go from pub to pub with his fiddle,' she says, 'from The Angel to The Antelope, then The Bear, a song for a drink. You can imagine how popular he was. He drank his wages into the bargain. And on top of his wages, he was paid as well for weddings and funerals but still he came home broke and drunk. That's why we had lodgers. He wasn't like he is now.'

We took this for one of Mom's many exaggerations, this shuffling man with the round glasses, half silent, fully compliant. She tells us more later and worse, but he is old and senile by then, picking turnips out of his bedroom carpet, and it's even more difficult to believe.

In the summer, Nan shoos us into the garden to help her with the rockery.

'That flower there with the little pink petals, that's London Pride. And this is rosemary. And this is thyme, you can use that on chicken. Some people would even use it in a jelly,' she says, making it sound like a novel idea and yet completely beneath her.

She pulls at the weeds with her arthritic hands and gives us little jobs picking up leaves and sweeping the path. She makes all the jobs into a list and puts Kim in charge of us and tells us to do them one by one and to take our time and do it properly because she'll come out and check, but really we know it's so that she can take Mom inside for tea and gossip. They cover the neighbours, Mom's brothers and their wives, the outstanding successes of the white cousins, the daughter in Australia, the son in South Africa, Ireland in general, Wexford in particular. They have their own version of a mother-and-daughter heart-to-heart centring on the virtues and secrets of food rejuvenation or how to make a meal stretch beyond its natural length. Nan is mistress of the stretch.

'You'll never have a stale loaf if you sprinkle it with a little water and heat it through, Sheila. In a warm oven, now.'

'Take your tomato ketchup and when it's finished add a drop of milk and sugar and a good shake, Sheila.'

'Look now, watch, Sheila. Vinegar will stretch that brown sauce. There's inches left in that bottle.'

And the catch-all: 'Mash it up and put it in with the potatoes, Sheila.'

As soon as the women go inside, Grandad wanders out with a little stool, sits down and plays the fiddle for us while we wander around and wait to go home.

Other times when we visit Nan she's in a good mood, laughing and joking, with her sharp observations on life. Mom and Nan are discussing the Donnellys, a Dublin family with two identical boys and a big car who have their house up for sale. Nan calls them 'Kiss and Scratch' because of their famous public arguments. And Peggy Donnelly has a way with her net curtains that infuriates Nan.

'She's extravagant,' Nan says. 'And she's a good few degrees above herself.'

'They reckon the area's going downhill and they want to move up to Solihull,' says Mom, who's half convinced that the going-downhill of Moseley is something to do with us.

'Do they now?' says Nan with a sniff. 'Well, the rates up there will put manners in that one.'

No matter how hard it is, Mom knows that she needs to tell her mother about the good news of the Kingdom and try to save her from Catholicism before Jehovah's War comes and reveals the apostasy of the Pope and all the nuns and priests at St Anne's.

She starts at an oblique angle.

'Did you see there was an earthquake in India, Mom? It was on the news.'

'I did.'

'They're coming quicker now, aren't they? There's always some disaster somewhere in the world.'

'And there always was,' says Nan, because she knows every move on the chessboard.

'After Armageddon we won't have any more wars or conflict. And sickness as well. And old age. And there'll be lots of food for everyone. Don't you think that's lovely?' It comes out in an untidy scramble, in a begging voice, a child who wants her mother's love.

'Armageddon now, is it?' says Nan.

'Yes, Jehovah's organization gives us warnings. It's all in *The Watchtower.*'

'Ah, Sheila,' says Nan, eyes in the corner of her sockets, 'you shouldn't believe everything you read. Paper never refused ink.'

It's a push-me-pull-you of a dance, old as time, the child who was never the favourite, the mother who couldn't love enough. They lock in with clumsy footsteps, out of step to the music, each one trying to lead, stepping on toes.

13

A Cup of Tea

One Sunday, when I am eleven, we walk from the Kingdom Hall around the corner to Nan's house. Mom is bursting to tell her the news.

'Aidan's asked the girls to be bridesmaids,' she says.

Nan says nothing while she takes this in. This is news indeed. She makes a pot of strong tea in the big brown pot and puts it on the table. She puts down a cup and a saucer and places the biscuit tin between them on the table. Lid on.

My mother takes her cup of tea and she's a different woman sipping it. Proud, she is. This will be a big affair: the last wedding of the Doyles, the youngest boy and my mother's favourite. She was fifteen when Aidan was born and she'd practically brought him up and this cemented the love they had for one another. Not only that. Here was confirmation of her special place in his affections and she brimmed with importance and relief. We were being asked not just as audience but as participants, playing a big part, the brown children, the black father. We would all be there.

When she told Dad the day before, she picked her words carefully.

'They'll be bridesmaids, Arthur. It's lovely of him to ask the girls, isn't it? He could have had anyone.'

We already knew Dad's views on public occasions. His advice always centred on his one abiding maxim: 'You better behave. You have the eyes of the white man on you.'

Nan is quick to pour cold water on my mother's joy.

'What about the dresses? They'll not be cheap,' she's says with narrowing eyes. She's heard all about the unyielding wallet of my father.

'Aidan's paying for them. The girls have got to go to Northfield to get measured and there's a seamstress making them up.'

'I see,' Nan sniffs. By rights, family information of this stature should have come first to Margaret Doyle, where it would have been examined, picked over and modified according to what would look best on the wedding photos, and that would not, under any circumstances, be the O'Loughlin children.

'And there's little pink muffs,' Mom continues un-daunted, 'and pretty little flower things for their hair. I've seen the design. It's beautiful.'

'And shoes?' Nan is quick to pounce on my mother's pause. 'Shoes, Sheila,' she says, rapping the table. 'Have you told your husband they'll need shoes? Four pairs no less. White ones.'

Mom nods. 'I know.'

Nan lays a motherly hand on her daughter's arm. 'Leave it with me, Sheila. I'll see what I can do.'

Mom's quiet on the way home, caught as she is between the meanness of her husband and the shame of having to take her mother's help. She often tells us the names her mother called her when she learned of her pregnancy for a black man. She counts off by unfolding her fingers one at a time. 'Whore. Dirty bitch. Disgrace. Prostitute. Jezebel. Tramp . . .'

Mom never runs out of words, but she always stops after a while and stares off into space.

'She was ashamed of me. Once she said, "Aren't you disgracing yourself when you come down to it, Sheila? I didn't come here to be made a laughing stock."'

And then she tells us about the teachers at English Martyrs' Junior School tying her left hand behind her back, bending her devilish wilfulness to the curve of the alphabet and godly right-handedness.

'I couldn't write for weeks,' she says. 'Made me feel terrible, that did,' she says, as though she's back there, half believing their superstitions.

Nan's rare visits to our house are on the strict understanding that my father will be at work, that she won't have to sit down with the beast and make conversation. That's if he can talk English at all, which was always very much in doubt. Occasionally she gets it wrong and Dad comes home when she's still drinking tea in the kitchen, and when she hears him in the hall, she stands and buttons her coat.

'I have to be going now, Sheila. The bus.'

'Maggie,' my father says when he sees her. 'You keeping all right?'

'Oh yes,' she says, taking the long passage at a trot, barely breathing until she's safely out on Springfield Road waving goodbye. My mother makes excuses for her.

'She only came to bring some wool/knitting/bacon/ needles/messages/cake.'

And my father shakes his head at her shame.

Months go by. The absence of the shoes becomes an urgent talking point. We've been measured and fitted for our pink satin dresses that hang upstairs under cellophane. Our little pink muffs dangle from silky pink cord and our glittering tiaras are stacked together on Mom's dressing table. No shoes.

A few weeks before the wedding, Nan arrives, breathless, in the kitchen.

'I'm as good as my word, Sheila. Didn't I tell you I'd find something for the girls?'

Mom makes Nan a cup of tea in a proper cup and sends Dean sprinting to the shop for biscuits.

'Thanks, Mom,' she says with her hand splayed over her heart.

We gather round as Nan opens her shopping bag. There are no shoeboxes, just plastic bags wrapped around something inside. She passes each bundle carefully to Mom, who sits down opposite her mother.

'I went to the Rag Market,' Nan continues, tapping the table between them. 'If you can't find a bargain in that place, there's none to be had. I walked up and down, up and down, until I found them.'

Mom unwraps each package in turn and places the contents on the table in front of her. These are not shoes, these are pumps, gym shoes. They are second-hand. They are dirty and grey and scuffed and laceless and worn down at the back and ugly.

Mom stares and stares and we look at her face sagging under the weight of confirmation. Nan looks from the shoes to Mom's face and back to the shoes. She picks them up and turns them over one by one.

'They'll do, they'll do. Sure, aren't the dresses long enough to cover them? Nobody will see them, Sheila. What are you worrying about? They're grand, aren't they? You can get some of the white stuff that you paint on. You can bleach out any stains and they'll be as good as new.'

The next day, Mom shouts us all awake and tells us to get dressed. Excited voice, strong and certain.

'Hurry up! We're going into town. Shopping!' she says, pulling the belt on her brown coat. 'All of you, downstairs! Hurry up!'

We get off the number 91 bus and walk straight into Start-Rite.

'I want four pairs of white shoes,' she says confidently, her hand grasping the handle of her shopping bag. 'It's for a wedding. They're going to be bridesmaids.'

The other customers turn and look, and Mom for a change meets their eye and nods. 'My brother,' she says to no one, to everyone. 'Youngest brother. And these are my children.'

We are measured and we are waited on. My shoes are new, they are glittery and princess white with a pretty bow at the front. Tracey's are the same and because Kim is older, hers are a bit different, with a little heel. Karen's are pretty and dainty with glitter and a single pearl button. They cannot be passed from one girl to the next. They cannot be worn for school. They will be no good in the rain, in the park, in the garden. We walk proudly out of the shoe shop, each of us swinging our own bag.

Only when we get home and Mom tells Dad how much it all cost do we realize the depth of the insult that Nan had dealt him.

'Good,' he says. 'Go tell Maggie the price.'

14

Proper Dinner on a Proper Plate

'Kim! Mandy! Tracey! Dean! Karen!'

Hysterical voice, crazy with high notes of happy. Sometimes hysterical voice is crazy with notes of despair. This is when she's lost her purse and it's time for the meeting. Or she's lost her bus pass, the one that gives her free travel because she married a bus driver. When you hear this voice, it means you have to come and help her tip out the ironing basket in case it's in there or go out to look in the garden in case it's on the path or walk out on to Springfield Road in case she dropped it and it's still unaccountably lying there. While we're looking, she starts to cry and prays out loud to Jehovah to help her find it, and when Dean or Kim or Tracey discover it in the kitchen drawer where we keep hairbrushes and combs, she thanks Jehovah for guiding their vision and persistence. We don't believe he's got time to help her find her purse because he's busy directing the faithful to the homes of the non-believers, but we can't say anything.

On this day, she calls and calls, and wherever we are in the house we go to her knowing we're not going to get a telling-off. Something exciting is going to happen.

'Sit down! All of you! Come on,' she says. 'Sit down. Pens and pencils. Coloured pencils. I just bought them. New. There's lots there. Move over. Kim make room for Tracey. Let Karen see, let her watch you. Make some space. She's only little. Look, colouring books! One each. I just bought them. Sit down and just draw. Draw whatever you like! That's all you have to do today. Draw.'

She's pulled the table right into the middle of the room so we can all sit around it at the same time. Her eyes are shining and she's all eager, jittery, dancing from child to child. And as soon as you pick something up, she's taking it out of your hand and giving you something else. There's plasticine in every colour and sharpened pencils, colouring books, rulers and glue, a stapler, felt pens, little watercolour paint sets from Ace Value, set squares and compasses. She's spent a fortune.

She spreads a roll of wallpaper from one end of the table to the other and turns it over.

'You can use this side. Look! It's fantastic! You can't ever run out! Look!'

She unrolls it like a circus performer and it falls across the table and on to the floor. She picks it up and rolls it back, folds it back, over and over, until there's a concertina wad, some of it plain and porous, some of it glossy blue leaves with silver birds that should be on the wall of one of the posh houses in Solihull.

'Watch! Hold this!' she says.

She dashes a whole two yards to the kitchen drawer and gets a carving knife. Runs back brandishing it in the air.

'Just watch!'

She traps her tongue between her teeth and slips the knife between the folds and slices against the edge, quick and deft, the long blade flicking and nicking until the wallpaper becomes sheets of normal paper on the table, more than we could ever use. She picks one piece up and starts folding it this way and that.

'You could make things, shapes or fans or . . . paper lanterns. You could cut things out. Wait! I'll get the scissors. Where are they? Where are the scissors?' She's rummaging in drawers and turning round and round in the kitchen.

'Scissors! Has anybody seen the scissors? The big wall-paper scissors. Don't say we've lost the scissors. Where did you last see the scissors? Where are they?'

The scissors appear with Jehovah's help and we can breathe again.

We can't start until she leaves us alone, until she stops directing our fun. Once she bought a huge trunk from a jumble sale and filled it with saris and jerkins, with felt hats and tweed coats, with tapestry waistcoats and leather shoes that curled up at the toe, with little pixie boots and leather bags. She comes home sometimes with strange things she's found in second-hand shops: a violin, ballet shoes, a machine for winding wool, knitting needles, medals, a wooden box that smells of tobacco. She comes home with chairs and curtains and measuring spoons, with clothes that she embroiders and cuts to fit, clothes that suit younger women who go to pop concerts and wear flowers in their hair.

Eventually, when she's sure we have covered every single idea and possibility, when we have every single thing we could ever need and more, when she's shown us everything she's bought and we know nothing has been left out, she stands back and watches us crowd in, picking things up and looking for the best picture in our colouring books.

But she hasn't finished.

'Or stories!' she shouts. 'What about stories? Bible stories? Any stories! Make things up!'

She makes herself a space and leans on the table. She picks up a pen and starts writing something and then suddenly she stops.

'I'm going to make you a lovely dinner!'

We look from one to the other. We say nothing. We have been here before and she will need to go right to the end of the line. She clears the sideboard of the things that have gathered over weeks: hairbrushes, newspapers, a baby's bottle, a vest, plastic cups, blue and pink dummies, soap powder, an empty jam jar, the button box. The kitchen is always a mess. She loads everything on the draining board for later. She wipes down the work surfaces. She empties the mop bucket that's always full of dirty water. She wrings the mop and hangs it upside down to dry.

She's singing. She's whistling. She's banging things and making a noise. She's doing everything at double speed. She boils both kettles and pours the boiling water into the sink, she throws everything in and out comes the bleach, the Vim, the Brillo pads. A cloth is thrown over her shoulder, there's another one gripped in her hand. She picks up tea towels at random and rips them in half for cleaning cloths. The kitchen is being transformed around us. And while she cleans, she keeps nipping over to see what we're doing.

'Kim! That's lovely! Look at that!'

She picks up Kim's picture, hand drawn, freestyle, a knight on a horse.

'You're so clever. I never used to have pens and pencils when I was little. Your nan wouldn't let us draw and I vowed, when I had kids, they'd have time to just sit and draw. Just draw and play and dress up. That's what I wanted for my children, all the things I never had. Mary was Mom's favourite. Not me.'

We've heard it before. We've heard about her, second of nine children, looking after the seven children who came after her as well as the lodgers, as well as helping with the housework, as well as tidying up, as well as going to Mass, as well as going to school to be bullied for being Irish, as well as being the one who Nan didn't love and the one who Grandad ignored. We know it off by heart.

'That's it, colour inside the lines, Mandy. Dean, you are so artistic! Isn't he artistic? Lovely, Tracey. Make room for Karen, let her join in. There you are, Karen, love. You play with the plasticine. Kim, you help her.'

She stands over Kim and we all stop what we're doing to watch her squeeze the plasticine into a blue dog, a yellow cat, a tiny yellow mouse. Mom looks longingly at the little shapes.

'I would never be able to do that.'

But in half a moment she's singing again and tins of food appear on the side, always the same, a tin of cooked mincemeat and a tin of apple pie filling. She takes a deep breath.

'Pastry,' she says to herself. 'Come on, Sheila. You can do it.'

In my colouring book, I always choose pictures of flowers because there are lots of small petals and you can swap colours all the time. You don't get fed up just doing lots of yellow or green like if you have a soldier in a uniform that's just red all the time and you can see the lines of the pencil. I hate that.

We are all here together. No Bible. No Dad. No jobs. Mom is cooking. And if anyone came in, like a visitor or a neighbour or someone from the Kingdom Hall, they would think it was always like this. They would look at us and our tidy kitchen and Mom covered in flour and they would think we were normal, just like everyone else, like a family off the telly even.

But better still if they saw us when the meat pies come out of the oven, how she's made leaves and roses out of the leftover pastry, crimped the sides with thumb and forefinger and brushed the top with egg and milk, and then when they come out of the oven, oh when they come out, golden and steaming, and we've each got a fat slice with mash and tinned carrots so soft you can force them between your teeth and grin at your sister and she screams and says 'Stop it!'

Gravy with the meat pie, custard with the apple. One of us will have a plastic plate or a serving bowl because there's never enough crockery to go round and every random dinner plate has a blackened hairline crack or a chip, but it's a proper dinner on a proper plate with a proper knife and fork if we can find them and a spoon if not, and we are all sitting at the table with hot food like kids off the telly and Mom's in a good mood, humming something to herself, and for a couple of hours nothing else matters.

She never sits down and eats with us. She stands and watches and listens to us. She looks at the things we have made and if there's any pie left she cuts it into small pieces which she loads on to our plates even though there's no room in our bellies, even though we can hardly move.

'Why don't you have it, Mom?' I say.

'Not hungry,' she answers, walks away from the mess, wanders upstairs or into the garden. So we do too, plates left where they sit, all our drawings and stories fallen to the floor.

The next day her face is tight and Satan's voice has arrived.

'Get down here and tidy this bloody kitchen! Now!'

We lumber downstairs and pass her in the hallway.

'Look at the state of that room!' she hisses.

We scald the plates in boiling water to loosen the wrinkled skin of gravy or the scab of custard. I pick the old, cold pastry off the side of the tin, little bits of meat, little bits of fruit, and nibble them, wedge them under my tongue to soften them, plunge my hands wrist-deep in the washing-up water, grateful for the heat.

15

Everywhere Else It's Christmas

Everywhere else in the world it's Christmas. At 70 Springfield Road it's Wednesday 25th December. There are things
we mustn't say, words that will earn us a slap or a lecture,
a scripture or a look. Or sometimes all of them at the same
time. The words are:

Christmas or any abbreviation thereof
Virgin Mary
Saviour
Mistletoe
Presents
Turkey

Wise Men
Donkey
Joseph
Manger
Fairy
Star
Bethlehem
Tree
Hallelujah
Hymn
Carols
Church
Mass
Hosanna
Tinsel
Excitement

At least it's Wednesday. There are no meetings on Wednesdays so we don't have to walk to the Kingdom Hall. When Christmas Day falls on a Sunday or a Tuesday or a Thursday, we still have to go but because there are no buses running we have to walk all the way there and all the way back. Under no circumstances could the meeting be rearranged because then we would be acknowledging that 25th December was a special day. And it's not. We have the evidence to prove it. The house is entirely and completely empty of decorations, tree, presents, smells of cinnamon and mulled wine, warmth, fun, extra food, games and relatives. All we have to tell us that it's Christmas are the films on the telly, *The Great Escape, It's a Wonderful Life, The King and I.*

Conrad won't come round if he's got any sense. He'll be at home with his mom and the rest of his other family, and we know he'll have lots of food and maybe presents, and it makes all the absences in our house even harder to bear.

My father, who is not a Jehovah's Witness, makes one concession to the festive period. He makes enough Christmas cake to feed the whole of exiled St Kitts and starts his preparations in the middle of summer with The Soaking of the Fruit.

'Run down Stratford Road,' he says and the three of us take a shopping bag each and drag home packets and packets of dried fruit, blue-black raisins, golden sultanas, leathery prunes, pounds of the stuff. He sends Mom for demijohns of sweet sherry and rum from the off-licence and gathers everything together in the kitchen. She loves the industry and organization he commands and falls into line like she's one of us, a child doing as she's told.

He scalds five enormous Kilner jars and stands them steaming on the draining board. He opens the bottles of brandy and rum the hue of his skin and small corked bottles of a nameless liqueur that smells sickly sweet and reminds me of my father's barber.

Then he sharpens the kitchen knife on the back step, scraping it at an angle against the stone, back and forth, until the blade shines along its curved edge. He picks prunes from the packet and stones them with a swift curl of his wrist, then chops them into fine pieces against his palm, piling the bits into a big, sticky heap on the kitchen table.

We dare not moan when he gives us jobs, accompanied as always by his running commentary. One look would be enough from Dad. He never needs to shout, he never hits us, he just looks at us slow and calm with his yellowy eyes and starts his interrogation with the same phrase every time: 'Well, tell me something . . .' When you hear this, you know you're in trouble. But the cake affair, even though it takes all of the day and most of the night, is different because at the end there is cake and before that there is cake mixture.

'Line up the jars, line them up. Listen good. Now, take a bag of fruit each. Kim, you is raisins, Tracey, you is sultanas, Mandy, you is prunes. Take a handful, drop them in turn by turn, mix them up, go round each other, that's it, fill the jars, good, bit by bit, that's it, right to the top.'

We feign incompetence, messing up his system, making him reorganize us and explain again what he was trying to do. We take it to the wire, just enough to annoy him, not enough to get told off.

'You have to make sure you don't have too much of anything. Look here, too many raisins. Mandy, take it easy on the prunes, not so much, not so much.'

We know this is all for Christmas and it will be the only thing that will tell us that it's a special time, and sometimes the only thing we will have to eat at all, but it's such a long way off, we can't muster any interest.

'Listen good,' he says, picking up the bits we drop,

'when the cake is done, you want it just right, each one must have a little bit of everything, all the same.'

'Yes, Dad,' we say, flicking raisins behind his back.

My father fills the jars with pints of spirits, pouring some of each one into each jar like an apothecary, always dribbling some of it down the side so it pools at the base. We dip our fingers in, wincing and coughing as it burns our tongues.

Then he screws the lids tight and stows them in the far recesses of the pantry, underneath the stairs, where the fruit plumps and swells in the dark while Halloween and Guy Fawkes Night come and go and the trees are stripped bare.

The actual cake baking starts in the first week of December. Every year we shrink from the endless instructions and preparations.

The whole house is involved. First, we have to find every single baking pan, Pyrex dish or metal container we can. Then we have to make half-a-dozen trips to the shops for butter and eggs, vanilla essence, nutmeg, mixed spice, ginger, flour, sugar. It takes all day. Mom buys a big plastic bucket with a handle while he retrieves the wooden mixing bat from the pantry. It's long and thin, like a paddle, with a wide handle, brought out just once a year for this occasion.

When he starts, we have to help. No one is excused. We peel the paper off the butter and drop it into the bucket, crack the eggs, pour the sugar in straight from the packet while he beats and beats, his mighty arm going over and over like a machine, the bucket between his legs, his sleeves rolled to the elbow. His eyes never leave the mixture and we stand over him, each one with a spice.

'Nutmeg,' he says. We tip it in. He beats the mixture. Looks. Tastes.

'Vanilla essence, Tracey.' In it goes. He beats. Looks. Tastes.

'Ginger, Kim.' And again.

'More nutmeg . . .' And so it goes, endlessly, all of us together in the kitchen pressing forward to the end goal with a tip of this, a drop of that, the oven turned on to get warm and the tins greased and lined up on the side waiting for the precious mixture. When he's mixed pints and pints of the cake mixture, he stops and mops his brow. We wait for the order.

'Bring out The Fruits.'

We open the pantry door and go down three steps. Right at the back, we pick up a jar each and carry it with two hands into the kitchen and place it before him.

'Lids off.'

We do it.

'Get a spoon. A big spoon.'

We do it.

'Mandy, you can start.'

I dig the spoon into the jar and ladle in the fruits, fragrant and spicy and alcoholic. The fruits slip into the dark-brown cake mixture, disappearing into the batter while I shovel it on, spoon after spoon, until all of my jar is gone. Kim moves into place, doing the same while we watch, as Dad folds the fruit in and the colour turns from gold to mahogany and we're getting close to the end. More beating, more instructions, but we say nothing. We know what bounty awaits the patient.

The baking goes on into the night, one cake in, one out, the gas meter topped up with endless coins, and one of us has to sit and tend the oven like it's a baby with colic. But before then, the bucket is handed over and we descend on it like savages, wiping our fingers endlessly round the sides, slicking off the mixture and wiping it on our tongue, in again and again until the bucket is clean and we are sticky from head to toe.

We begin to dread the deliveries. When the cakes are cold, he double-wraps them in greaseproof paper, then aluminium foil, and packs them in a cardboard box, a dozen or more. He loads them and us into the back of his car and skids us through the winter streets to drop them off one by one. On the salted front doorsteps of narrow terraced houses, we stamp and shiver, one eye on the daggers of ice that dangle from the roof.

'Come in, come in! Come! Yes, come!'

It's a long day of visits to front rooms that look exactly like ours – a Dralon sofa, starched frilly coasters, cricket photographs, maps of the Caribbean, a blue glass fish ornament, an orange plastic pineapple waiting for ice and good times. We stand politely while Dad talks to his friends from back home, never fidgeting, never looking bored, never touching anything, anything at all. Or sometimes we hover in steamy kitchens exactly like ours, a big alu-minium kettle, a Dutch pot, flowery crockery and enough

Pyrex for a church fête. *Don't touch, don't speak, don't eat anything even if it's offered, don't interrupt.*

We listen to the same repeated stories about back home, where the sun shone and you felt it in your bones, we endure pinched cheeks and 'Look, how they've grown,' endless comparisons, endless measurements.

'Bless you, Arthur,' an old woman says. An old man with snowy hair and rheumy eyes balances on his walking sticks and shakes my father's hand. 'You never forget us, Arthur. All year we look out for you.'

The smell of rum and brandy, burnt sugar and spice clings to the curtains and cushions all the way through Christmas and into the New Year.

During the Christmas holidays we also go to visit Nan, who's got a Christmas tree and tinsel and decorations everywhere, but Nan can't mention Christmas to us or buy us presents because then her and Mom have an argument about the evils of the Catholic Church and its pagan rules and rituals like Mass and Confession. We wonder about our cousins and whether Nan buys them presents and if they visit her and open boxes tied with ribbon sitting under her sparkling tree, stuffed to bursting with mince pies and Quality Street.

Still, every year, around New Year, Mom gets all dressed up to go to the Talk of the Town with her brothers and sisters. It's dancing and dinner and a band and a comedian and more dancing, Mom with her sister Teresa doing the jive because she can still move, you know, and laughs and drinks and a singalong when they've all had one too many. She starts getting ready early in the day with a visit to the hairdresser for a curly perm. When she comes back, we have to say it looks nice or she gets upset. She's bought herself a new outfit and reminds everyone that it's only once a year.

'Once a year, I go out. Once a year. It's only right I spend a bit of money on myself.'

Sometimes Mom's brothers will bring their wives, but Mom doesn't even bother to ask Dad any more. There would be no point.

Late afternoon, she sends me across the road to Marg. Marg lives with Ken and their Dachshund, Candy.

'Mom said can she borrow some make-up. She's going to the Talk of the Town.'

Marg always has a cigarette in her mouth or between her fingers and has the make-up bag waiting by the front door.

'Crimson Dream, that lipstick is. Brand new. Tell her to take it with her for after she's had her meal. Tell her I've put the black pencil in instead of the brown because you need a bit of drama at night. And I've put in a little bottle of nail varnish if she's got time. And a bit of powder.'

Mom sits in the kitchen and assembles everything. I sit opposite to watch. The make-up smells womanly and exciting and I cannot wait to buy my own from Woolworths as soon as I'm allowed. She sits with a little mirror and takes her time with the eyeliner and lipstick. She dabs a little circular puffer on her cheeks.

Dad winks at us.

'You out to get yourself a fancy man, Sheila?'

'Might,' she says with a bitterness we've begun to expect. She's always tired these days and doesn't play along with Dad's jokes.

She looks thin in her 18 Hour Girdle and her seamed stockings. She shrugs on her coat, adds a little fur collar and snaps her handbag shut. She's got a great pair of legs in her black patent kitten heels. She's excited and we mill around her, fixing her hair at the back and spraying old perfume on her neck.

'I'll get a taxi back,' she says defiantly, baiting him, willing him to object. He says nothing, avoiding the inevitable row.

'Bye, then!' she calls from the front door and we watch her sashay down Springfield Road, off to the bright lights of Five Ways.

We're all still up when she comes home, tipsy.

'Got a proper black cab,' she says to underline the depth of her extravagance and winks in our direction because she knows Dad will hate it. He barely turns his head, but we watch her – slightly giddy, care-less, lighter somehow, all her edges blurred by Baileys Irish Cream.

'Oh, there was this comedian, Arthur. Irish bloke. Listen . . .' She has her thickest Irish accent on. 'Mary says to her husband, Paddy, "Now, Paddy, if you were stranded on a desert island, who would you most like to be with?" Paddy has a good long think. Eventually, he looks at Mary and he says, "Well, I think it would have to be my uncle Mick." Now Mary has a right face on her. It's not the answer she was expecting. "Really, Paddy," she says. "And what in God's name is so special about your uncle Mick?" "Ah well," says Paddy, "for a start, he has a boat.'"

Mom's laughing and we all laugh with her.

'That's the thing about Irish people, Arthur. We know how to laugh at ourselves.'

She staggers out of the room and up to bed, singing, *'Please release me, let me go.'*

In the morning, she'll take two Panadol and tell us the joke all over again.

16

Tramps and Sticklebacks

No school. We spend the whole of the six-week summer holiday in the back garden, a long strip of grass with a carpet-runner path that leads from the back door to the black iron railings that overlook the playing fields of Moseley School and the boys' grammar school beyond. We used to squeeze through a gap in the fence and play in the sandpit by the long jump in the playing fields. We could sit there for ages before the caretaker saw us and started shouting. We would stand up quickly and dash back through the hole and disappear into the house, laughing with fear and excitement. Then back again the next day, wandering around the grounds and looking for lost cricket balls, picking dandelions and blowing the seeds up to the sky to make a wish.

But all that's stopped because Mom's become a child-minder. The doorbell starts ringing at seven in the morning with people dropping their children off. Mom peels swad-dled babies out of their mother's arms with a practised twist. Mewling kids are chivvied and hushed, sleeping kids are never woken, and sniffling, snotty toddlers with scraps of sodden cloth are passed straight to one of us to take inside before they can realize what's happening. Screaming children who have cottoned on to the impend-ing parting are grasped tightly and clutched to Mom's chest.

'He'll be fine once you've gone,' Mom says in a West Indian voice for the West Indian mothers, an Irish voice for the Irish mothers and the idiot voice, one clipped word at a time, for the Africans and Asians.

'He. Will. Stop. Crying. When. You. Close. Door.'

All week our house is full of these kids. It smells of baby shit and milk vomit, of boiling nappies and pine disinfectant.

Me, Kim and Tracey have to feed and wash the babies, bring the wind up, amuse them, stop them crying, jiggle them on our hips and make sure they have whatever they need. Rosehip syrup for this one, rusks in milk for that one, formula with cold water for another. Change that nappy, wipe the yellow shit off with a corner of the cloth, wash again and again, softly because of the red-raw nappy rash, and if the shit has slid up the baby's back and into the soft folds of the neck, then it's the whole baby in the pink plastic bath with special baby soap and your elbow in the water to check for heat. Then cream the little rump, up into the private folds, a new nappy, a little play but not too much because there are other babies and other jobs. Get a new romper suit from the pile and dress the child, hopefully in its own clothes but not always. Down with that one for a nap, pick up another. Or a toddler with a sore knee or a running green nose. Endless care-taking while Mom's tidying and directing traffic.

No one can look after babies like my mom. She can have a fidgety baby relaxed and asleep in ten minutes. She nestles it into the crook of her arm and gets her face really close. She swaddles it and talks to it in a grown-up voice about going to sleep and everything being OK and, before you know it, the tiny face is looking at her and the blinks get slower until it surrenders into her, soft and safe. She can hear a cry at fifty paces and identify the baby and the cause.

'Listen. That's Kashif. He's hungry.'

Or, 'Go and see to Nicholas. He needs changing.'

She's got no time for spoilt children, but there's a pitch to a cry that always has her running, the baby who's scared or upset or wants his mom. Then she's all over it and no one else gets a look-in.

But on Saturdays and Sundays, when all the kids have gone, we get our house back and Mom orders us outside: anywhere will do – Sparkhill Park, the garden, someone else's garden – just don't be inside under her feet.

Sometimes we go to the rec at the top of the road where Sarehole Mill stands, a tall brick building where Tolkein used to go to write about Middle Earth. There's nothing at the rec, it's just the recreation park, but we all thought it got its name because it was the site of a shipwreck from when the river burst its banks and the ship got marooned. We told Mom once.

'Ship? We're hundreds of miles from the sea,' she said, shaking her head. '"Rec" means "recreation", not "wreck" with a "w".' But we were never sure of her facts and decided the shipwreck was still at least a possibility.

There are no swings at the rec, no slides, no round-about, no bandstand or shelter, but it has got a stream and a ford that cars drive through when the water level is low enough and two enormous oak trees that cast deep shade on a hot day.

We take margarine sandwiches and bottles of weak squash and we are gone all day, catching sticklebacks and putting them in jam jars, watching them go round and round in the murky water.

We tramp around the edges of the park where the long grass grows, where people lose balls and fishing nets, and we brush against stinging nettles and have to hunt for dock leaves to wipe on the bubbly rash that stains our brown skin a watery green.

We poke at lumpy frogspawn and squeal as unseen creatures brush against our feet as we fish. We make stepping stones and colonize little islands on the other side of the river and invent elaborate rules for our secret kingdom. We chase each other and give piggyback rides, we fight with stripped branches for swords and daisy wreaths for crowns. We lose ourselves, find ourselves, and when the sun starts to go down, when Dean and Karen are tired, when we're hungry and thirsty, when we have poured our sticklebacks away and think we won't get told off for coming home early, we wander back to her, to the kitchen and whatever we can find to eat.

We know what she does while we're away because it's what she always does at the weekend even when we are at home. She starts to tidy and clean. She mops like someone is paying her, like someone's watching and she has to do a good job. She's on a chain gang and the overseer has a rifle trained on her back. Everything she does is at a hundred and ten per cent, as though someone were saying, 'No, you can't do that.' Yes she can. She bites down on her tongue and gnaws on it while she fills the grey galvanized iron bucket to the brim. The chemicals hum and sting my nose. The stringy cloth mop is sunk in and wrung out over and over.

She pushes it hard against the lino floor, into the corners of the room, the chairs upended on to the table so she can get underneath. She starts in the kitchen, sweats her way down the hall and out on to the front step that she scours with a worn scrubbing brush wetted in the mop bucket, working into the concrete in tight little circles.

If I'm playing in the garden and dare to creep inside, she makes me help, tells me to wedge the back door open, then the kitchen door open, then the porch door and the front door, all of them, wedge them wide open so the summer wind can whip through the house and dry the floors. And through her breathless efforts, and whether I ask for them or not, she tells me stories of her hard life.

'I broke my nose when I was your age. That's why I look like this. Nothing I can do about it now. I was always ashamed of the way I looked, different to my sisters.'

She tells me jokes.

'Why is a dog like a tree? Because they both lose their bark when they're dead.'

She tells me jokes featuring the Irishman, the Englishman and the Scotsman and does all the accents. She tells me jokes in a West Indian accent, an American accent, a Pakistani accent. She becomes Spike Milligan in a squeaky voice and Harry Secombe in a bass and all the other

comedians off the telly. She laughs until she cries sometimes and then goes back to her jobs, the unfunny, endless
continuum of keeping the house from the inevitable filth
and chaos.

She sploshes the last of the mop water on to the front path
where it floods the front garden and across the pavement
and into the gutter, disappearing down the drain. I run
towards it and float a leaf on the surface, watch it drop into
oblivion.

When she's done, I tiptoe to the front garden to sit on
the wall. If I am quiet, no one will know, and if I don't
spend too long, no one will miss me. The others will be
playing somewhere and I can be alone, brain-idling, thinking whatever I want or nothing at all. I never tell anyone
about this time. I don't want to share it.

I watch the passengers on the bus, the people driving
the cars, the passers-by and neighbours. I like to see how
different people walk. Some men walk on their toes and
not their heels, with their hands in their pockets. They're
usually young. The old men take slow, deliberate steps
in overcoats and trilbies, marching but to a slower beat.
Some women have handbags lodged in the crook of their
arm and that arm waves right and left as they walk, like
the rudder of a boat. They have headscarves and lipstick
like Auntie Marge, they have little heels on their shoes that
scuff the pavement as they walk. Women with shopping
bags don't have lipstick or handbags but carry their load
with long arms, with their heads at an angle like they're listening to half of a conversation. I like to watch the Irishmen

who lodge in the houses at the top of the road when they walk home, how tired they are, how tired. I like to watch old people who are bent from the middle of their backs like there's a special hinge there that only starts working when you get past sixty.

I see roaming dogs and suspicious cats, brown birds, sparrows that never come close enough to catch. I see Dot open her front door across the road and slip her shiny blue handbag on the arm of her blue coat and settle her blue scarf round her neck. She wears very thick brown stockings that look like they're keeping her big legs from wobbling when she walks. She has black hair in luxurious waves and if she's wearing a hat, it's always a shade of blue like everything else. She's old but she hasn't got a husband, hasn't got a child, and lives all alone in a house like ours with lots of empty rooms and red carpet. Maybe, once upon a time, Dot had children and her house was filled with toys and untidiness, with a man who sat by the telly and got his dinner served to him on a tray. I am certain she has a piano but I don't know why. She bolts her gate and gives me a faraway smile that doesn't need any response.

Then the two men who live together at the top of the road come walking past. One is taller than the other, but they both walk with small steps. They have an Alsatian dog with black-brown shaggy fur, which they keep on a tight leash. When they moved on to Springfield Road, everyone kept talking about them.

'Have you seen those two?' Mom says to Dad.

'What two?'

'The two blokes that live together with the dog?'

My father looks back at the telly. 'The two of them is anti-man,' he says.

I don't know what Dad means by 'anti-man' but they are always really neat and tidy with clothes that are a bit young for them, black leather jackets with long fringes and flared trousers in blue or purple velvet. Both of them have black hair but the black changes – sometimes it's so black it's almost purple and sometimes it's just ordinary and very, very black. Something about the dog makes people extra suspicious of them. I don't understand why but people always mention the dog, nudge each other and then laugh.

The anti-men are walking on my side of the road, coming closer and closer. They walk like they're trying not to catch anyone's eye, talking quietly to each other with their eyes down. The tall one, who is also the oldest, is wearing stripy trousers that don't look great on him and it makes me feel sorry for both of them. I jump off the wall and pretend to be waiting for someone.

'Hello,' I say.

It's the small one that answers. 'Lovely day,' he whispers and there's a sort of gratefulness in his voice, like I'm someone doing him a favour. I watch them walk past our house and I follow them for a little while.

Back on the wall, I resume my watching. There's a new black family on the road, Mr and Mrs Bird, but Dad says they're Bajans who think they're too nice.

'Barbados people, some of them forget what colour they is.'

Mr and Mrs Bird have two girls who always wear

matching dresses and mostly those matching dresses are tartan. The girls are a bit younger than us and wear perfect white socks with little flowers round the ankles. The girls have their thick hair in red ribbons and matching coats. The girls walk in step with their mother and they all hold hands. Every Sunday the whole family goes to church and if we're not careful we end up at the same bus stop at half past nine in the morning and Mom has to talk to Mrs Bird, who likes to put Mom right in her special Barbados twang.

> *Mom:* Hope the bus comes soon, Hazel.
> *Hazel Bird:* It's due at nine thirty-three so it's not time yet.
> *Mom:* It's just so cold, isn't it?
> *Hazel Bird:* That's what it's like in December.
> *Mom:* Your girls look lovely in them check coats.
> *Hazel Bird:* [Looks at Mom's substandard children, looks away without comment.]
> *Mom:* They grow up fast, don't they?
> *Hazel Bird:* They're children, that's what they do.
> *Mom:* Oh, look, here's the bus! At last!
> *Hazel Bird:* It's early, Sheila.

The Birds always sit right up at the front like they're desperate to get off and go and worship the Lord at their special Moravian Church while we would have stayed on the red plastic seats of the number 91 until the end of time if it meant we didn't have to go to the meetings for two very long hours.

Mr Bird is as unlike my father as it is possible to be. He has a sort of ginger, bushy moustache and his coat is old-fashioned. My dad wouldn't be seen dead in that sort of coat. Mr Bird isn't even allowed to hold the money for the bus fares. He isn't the boss of Mrs Bird and that's a fact. He walks a little bit behind her, he doesn't speak and his unruly moustache never moves. I sometimes see Mrs Bird without him but he is never, ever without her.

Until the Birds I didn't know there were posh black people. I thought everyone was like us.

I sit on the front-garden wall for hours. The road is like a film sometimes, a very slow film without any guns or fights, but their absence just makes it more interesting. In the emptiness of the street without cars and buses, I look at the front doors and think about the lives behind them, lives that nobody else can imagine. There's someone having an argument in a kitchen and maybe a baby crying in an upstairs room. There are people sitting and reading the newspaper and maybe someone is reading an airmail letter like the ones Mom gets from her sister in Australia. There are pictures of fields and lakes and rainbows hanging on walls and photographs of grandchildren and maybe someone died in the war and their photo is still on the mantelpiece so they are never forgotten. Someone is making a cake, someone is making a bed, someone is crying at a black-and-white film, someone is patting a dog. And if you speed up the film and cut out all the quiet bits it's even more interesting because then you would concentrate on all these people walking up and down the road.

People are different before they see me. When they think they're all alone on the road, they are wondering about things, private things, personal things, secrets, and

KIT DE WAAL

their eyes are staring straight ahead but seeing the moving pictures of their memories and thoughts inside their heads. But when they see me and know I'm watching, they make tiny, tiny adjustments to their walking, their eyes blink and they come back to the street from wherever they were and they smooth down the lapels of their coat or straighten a collar. The collar doesn't need straightening. We both know that and the lapels are just fine. It's a way of saying, 'I've seen you and you've seen me.'

They hardly ever speak, but they don't have to – I know that because of me they have changed ever so slightly, in a way that no one else would notice. But I notice and that makes garden-wall-watching time the best time of the day.

A little way up Springfield Road there is a large green-and-white Victorian farmhouse where Mr and Mrs Seacole live. They have a big car that's falling to pieces. I watch them get out and go inside. They don't speak to us. From their tall bedrooms they must be able to see across the allotments to the turrets of the grammar school where the posh and clever boys go from all over Moseley and Hall Green. Once upon a time, all of Springfield Road and Passey Road and Dovey Road and Tenby and Greenstead Road used to belong to the farmhouse, but it was sold so that little houses could be built for little people back when the world was black and white, before the television was invented.

Here comes Maggie May, the oldest woman in the world, striding down the road with a feather in her magnificent hat, a purple coat that drags on the floor, black-and-white-check tights and two red circles on her cheeks like she's on her way to the circus. When she passes, she tosses her long grey curls and inclines her head.

'I am to the shops the day,' she says, not exactly to me but there isn't anyone else.

I take a step backwards because she moves for no one. She carries an ornate walking stick that she bangs on the pavement, twice, like she's conjuring a spell.

She points it down towards Stratford Road – 'To the shops!' – and strides on.

Then just at the curve of the road, there's a new person I've never seen before, a tramp. He is bent over, grasping a short wooden walking stick. He's in dark-brown rags, wearing massive shoes like Charlie Chaplin, an old buckled hat that looks like someone stepped on it balanced on the back of his bald head, and he has coats on top of coats and a scarf that is mostly tears and holes. He's like something from a midnight movie, someone who might beg at a street corner holding out a gloved claw for a tossed coin or hide in a dark alley and jump out and scare people.

He's so bent I can't see his face, but he's coming close. I retreat into the front garden to let him go past, but he doesn't pass. He stands at the gate and comes towards me. I back off into the house.

'Mom! Mom!'

She comes from the kitchen with a tea towel in her hand.

'Hello,' she says and has the read of him immediately.

'Missus,' he replies, 'would you have a drink of water?'

'Come in. Sit down.'

I look at her. She's just mopped the hall and kitchen

and this man smells like a bin. We don't know him. Why does she do this? She's always talking to people who don't need talking to, strange people or mad people who everyone else avoids, old people that take forever to get to the point. That's why she takes so long to get the shopping. Sometimes when we're down Stratford Road, she'll just say a couple of words to someone and, before you know it, it's a long, long conversation that goes on forever and all you want to do is go home. Here she is again, talking to someone, but this time she's taking it too far. Other people don't have tramps in the house, why do we?

He shuffles through and I follow in his wake. The stench is unholy. He sits just inside the kitchen door with his legs spread, both hands on his stick. His face is filthy.

'Or a cup of tea,' he says.

My mother whistles and hums and I dash past the old man and into the garden.

'There's a tramp in the kitchen!'

We crowd around the back door. Even from here we can smell him. We watch Mom give him a cup of tea. She makes him a sandwich with food she has bought for us. She cuts it in half and hands it to him on a plate, but he whips it off and stuffs the whole thing in his mouth and starts muttering. It doesn't sound like 'thank you.'

'Have you come a long way?' she asks, folding her arms. 'It's hot out there. Are you on your way home? Do you live around here?'

We catch the odd word. They are all 'fuck.'

As he drinks his tea, he looks about. 'Who lives here with you, missus?'

'My husband and my children.'

'Big fucking house,' he says.

'Not with five of them,' she says, smiling as though she's on Stratford Road chatting to one of the clean and reasonable neighbours.

He eyes her through the filthy slits above his nose. 'Have you got a shilling, missus?'

She takes her purse out and hands him a coin. 'What's your name?'

'Morgan,' he says. 'I sleep where I sit.'

We take a collective gasp. Could she go so far as to let him sleep, to let him stay like the children who she looks after? Could she let him sleep where he sits and stink out the entire house and eat all our food? We wait to see what she'll do.

'Well,' she says. 'I've got my jobs to do today, Mr Morgan. I'll help you up.'

He takes ages to stand, huffing, puffing and swearing. He hands her the mug and shuffles off down the hallway. When he gets to the gate, he turns suddenly, eyeing us all, and we scuttle back inside to the front-room window to watch him go.

'He stinks, Mom,' I say.

'Not everyone can have a bath whenever they want. You don't know what happens to people. One day you can have everything and the next day, bad luck strikes. He'll have a story, that one.'

She opens all the windows and wafts a tea towel around the kitchen. She gets the mop bucket out again and adds some bleach.

'Out! Out!' she says. 'Go and play.'

He comes back, Mr Morgan, every couple of months. He raps the front door with his stick and just walks in. Mom gives him tea in a cup that none of us will ever touch again and a sandwich on a plate that is dead to us.

The end comes when me and Dean are in the kitchen and Mom is tidying up. Mr Morgan is on the chair by the door. He looks at us for a long time as he chomps through his food.

'Whose are the niggers?' he asks.

'What did you say?' says Mom.

'The little niggers. Who do they belong to?'

My mother walks over to him and brings him to his feet.

'Up you get,' she says. She walks him to the front door and slams it behind him.

She takes his mug and plate into the garden and smashes them against the brick wall.

'Cheeky sod,' she says.

17
You is Singing!

There's only one warm room in the house. It's the room that belongs to my father. The telly room. A huge brown Dralon chair sits at a perfect angle to the telly. It's my father's chair and it remains empty even when he's not in the house. Against the long wall is a beige three-seater sofa that's sunk in the middle with a loose arm and a few paper-thin cushions in mock velvet. There's a threadbare rug on the lino and thick curtains to keep out the sun so Dad can watch his films without any glare on the screen.

If you don't want to freeze elsewhere in the house, you sit with Dad. If you sit with Dad, you watch the telly. If you watch the telly, you watch Dad's choice. If it's Dad's choice, it's a black-and-white film, it's a detective show, it's the cricket, it's a Daddy Detective, that is to say American, that is to say slow, that is to say featuring an unlikely hero – a fat man, a scruffy man with a mangled cigar, a man in a wheelchair, a blind man, a nomad. Dad doesn't so much watch the telly as consume it, devour it, live through it. Silence is absolute. If you cough, you leave the room. If you speak, you leave the room. If you fidget, you leave the room. If you moan, you leave the room. He doesn't ask you to leave the room, he just swivels his head in your direction and when his eyes settle on you, as slow and certain as a laser, you get up quietly and close the door behind you. Never plead for mercy, never huff and blow, and under no circumstances, but never, ever attempt to kiss your teeth in his hearing. Those are the rules.

When it comes to films, he knows everything. And we must know what he knows. Halfway through *Gone with the Wind* he turns from the screen and speaks to all five of us stuffed together on the sofa.

'Who was Clark Gable married to?'

'Carole Lombard, Dad.' Any one of us answers.

'Good. And?'

'Died in a plane crash.'

His silence means you've got it right.

Or, 'You see Olivia de Havilland? Who she is?'

'Sister of Joan Fontaine, Dad.'

'And who is the man there?'

'Montgomery Clift.'

'Good.'

And we must know the name of every black actor and every film they are in. Woody Strode, Hattie McDaniel, Sidney Poitier, Harry Belafonte, Dorothy Dandridge, Paul Robeson, Sammy Davis Junior, Pearl Bailey.

It's not enough to watch, either. We must follow the plot, anticipate the end, appreciate the twist. We have to notice the things he notices.

'You see he put the money in the safe? Watch.'

'You see she put the gun in she bag? Watch.'

'Watch what happen to the boat.'

'Watch when she break the bottle of wine.'

We learn under his eye to deconstruct a film even while it's happening, why Cary Grant loves Ingrid Bergman enough to break into the Nazi mansion, why Alec Guinness builds the bridge over the River Kwai, why Jimmy Cagney goes to the electric chair screaming for his mother. Watch.

And we consume everything too, inhabit the wet streets of Brooklyn, the Russian steppes, the churned fields of Belgium and France. All under his eye. The midnight movie with Frankenstein's ragged monster stumbling through the forest pursued by the villagers; Sunday afternoon on a station platform with a middle-aged woman falling in love with a stranger in *Brief Encounter*; we eat our way through the humiliation of Olivia de Havilland in her Washington Square drawing room, the madness of Gregory Peck in

Moby Dick, the straining white chariot horses in *Ben Hur*. We get it, we know why he lives inside the telly because we do it too. We escape the little house on Springfield Road, the cold inside and the cold outside and the news and the neighbours and his job and our school and the meetings and the whole world.

Sometimes, without warning, he will dig into his trouser pocket and pull out a five-pound note.

'Dean, run down to the shop, get a block of ice cream. Vanilla.'

Dean is up and in his shoes before the words are out of his mouth.

'Kim, you and Tracey go and buy some Mackeson from the off-licence. Two bottles. No, better make it three. Them know you, you tell them is for you dad. They will give it to you. Run.'

I go with him into the kitchen to get the big metal coffee pot and find whatever cups and glasses I can. We hover around him like bees while he mashes the ice cream with a fork and loosens it with the dark, treacly stout. He sprinkles in nutmeg and vanilla essence, he mashes it again and again and adds condensed milk, sweet and pale, until it's a thick, sticky, alcoholic punch that he measures into our waiting cups.

'You can't have too much of this, Arthur boy,' he says to himself. 'You diabetes don't like it.'

But he leaves a good few inches in the metal pitcher that he carries back to the telly to catch the end of something we've seen or the beginning of something we haven't. We sip the nectar, never wanting it to end, but Dad opens the lid of the pot and drinks with long, loud gulps, the creamy froth like a white moustache on his upper lip.

One Sunday, we're watching a film with Dad. It's not very good, something we've seen before, a cowboy film in black and white with little Audie Murphy on a white horse or Randolph Scott with his sideways hat, where the bad guys are very bad and the good guys are too good and we've guessed the end before it's halfway through. My father has done an excellent job with our cinematic education and we are too discerning and easily bored.

We sit in a row on the sofa, wedged together, half dozing in the warm, dark fug. Audie Murphy does some horse stunts with a lasso while Dad tells us, again, about what this Hollywood star did in the Second World War.

'He was a war hero, you know. Audie Murphy get all the medals,' he says. 'Fight off the Japanese and the Germans them. Good soldier he was. He get wounded and everything, still carry on fighting. Famous soldier. Brave man, he was.'

'Yes, Dad,' we murmur.

He stops suddenly and jerks his chin to the kitchen.

'Listen!' he whispers.

Mom is singing. Not the ordinary tidying-up-the-kitchen singing but the performance of a lifetime. It's 1956, she's Ella Fitzgerald, Live at the London Palladium. Without even seeing her, we know the look in her eyes, the sparkly, faraway, somewhere-else-ness of her, the angle of her head, the size of her open mouth.

He stands and walks to the television, turns down the volume and then tiptoes towards the door with the burglar's step. He pulls the handle and puts his finger on his lips, his eyes narrow with devilment. Through the slender crack we listen. Dad is smiling. He picks up his newspaper and rolls it into a baton.

'Shhhh,' he says. 'Watch!'

She's coming to a crescendo when Dad yanks the door open and goes running into the kitchen. We are on his heels. Mom stands stock-still; the lyrics die on her lips.

Dad has the newspaper high in the air. 'Where is he? Sheilo! Where is he?'

'Who?' she shouts, looking around the kitchen.

'Let me get him for you, Sheilo!'

She stares at him. 'What is it, Arthur?'

'Who attack you?' He makes a show of going to the back door and opening it, of looking around inside the cupboards and behind the chairs.

'Me can't see him!'

Mom lowers her head and stands in the middle of the kitchen with her five children watching and Dad shakes his head as though the penny has finally dropped.

'Ohhhhh!' he says, lowering his weapon. 'Ohhhh! You is singing! I thought someone did attack you. But it was singing you was doing. Ohhh!'

He's laughing, a rippling belly laugh. It's so funny. We're with him, in on the joke. And we're with her, humiliated, half his size, red-faced, crying silently.

'Come,' he says to us. 'The film nearly done. You missing the best bit. I had to just make sure your mother wasn't being murdered by an intruder. What a noise she was making, eh?'

He winks as he walks past us back to his chair by the radiator. We cannot bear to follow him. We cannot bear to stay with her. We slink upstairs to other games.

18

x is Unknown

Kim always oversleeps. She stays up all night reading by the light of the lamp post outside. She pulls the curtains apart and turns the pages while Tracey sleeps and I watch. When the lights go off at midnight, she carries on, reading by whatever light she can find, a lamp with a naked bulb, a candle. Sometimes I ask her about her book, but she doesn't talk to me because whatever she's reading is more interesting or she doesn't even hear me because she's gone where the books take her, far away from me.

It's always a fat book, it's always old, something from a jumble sale or the library, and when she's finished, it's gone, it leaves the house and another one takes its place. She reads the Bible and she reads the Jehovah's Witness books, magazines, anything she can get her hands on. So, every morning, she won't wake up for school and eventually Mom tells me to go without her.

Sleeplessness is my nightly companion. Even after Kim has gone to sleep, dreaming of wizards and dwarves and children who go to boarding school and little women, I'm still awake.

I watch the bus headlights move across the ceiling; they start in one corner and paint an arc of light all the way to the other corner. The lights keep me company. I hear the cars coming from far, far away. I hear them change gear at the island at the bottom of the road, and then change gear again when they get to the corner of the road and drive past. Different cars have different sounds, taxis are different, buses are different again, and motorbikes and lorries and vans.

On summer nights there are people walking home late and I listen to them talking, laughing, singing songs. Sometimes a man will stop under the lamp post across the road and argue with his girlfriend.

'Fucking hell, Debbie. Give it a rest.'

'But, Mark—'

'But Mark what? What? I said fucking leave it!'

He needs the light to see his words land on her face. After a while, when she stops answering back, they walk on and I wonder about what will happen when they get home.

There are animals too. A lonely dog. A fox. A wailing cat that sounds like a baby crying. When my sleeplessness is really bad, I hear all this and then the birds start. One chirrup at first, a distant whistle, then more and more as it becomes lighter until Dad gets up for an early shift. His bedroom door opens and I hear him go to the toilet. After a while, the front door slams and the metal tips of his shoes ring out on the pavement and disappear down Stratford Road. Then, as soon as my eyes close, Mom is calling me for school, shaking me sometimes.

'Get up. It's half seven.'

The only reason we go to Waverley Grammar School is because Dad wouldn't let Kim go to Dame Elizabeth Cadbury, the art school that offered her a scholarship.

'Art? You can't do nothing with drawing,' he says when the letter arrives. Mom did the application form in secret because she knows how clever Kim is.

She's always telling people about how Kim knows everything about dinosaurs and history and how good her drawings are and how she's top in all her subjects and knows the answers to every question. Mom tries in a hundred different ways.

'They do all the rest as well, Arthur. Maths and English and everything. It's just that, with her talent, they'll know how to help her get better. They've got all the best teachers.'

'Art?'

'Yes and—'

'Where it is?'

'Bourneville. She can get the bus. Two buses.'

'Why she can't do the drawing at home?'

'We have to sign the papers this week, Arthur. We're running out of time.'

So they miss the deadline and the only grammar school with a space for Kim is Waverley Grammar School on the other side of the city, two long bus journeys away. Three sometimes. And where Kim goes, I must follow. But this morning, I have to make my way by myself.

I walk to the bus stop at the bottom of the road with my satchel and PE bag and let the first bus go by in case Kim comes. I'm torn between making the long journey on my own and my anxiety about being late and getting told off. I keep looking up the road but no Kim. It's raining this morning. I'm on my own and I'm hungry. Mom gave me some toast but I was too tired to eat it so I had tea with three sugars and a bite of the crust. I regret it now.

The bus comes sizzling along the wet road and I hop on. It's wide open at the back where the conductor stands, two straps across his chest, one for the ticket machine and one for the money.

Mom tells us all about how she used to let her friends off with their fares when she was a conductress. You could let them ride for free and then, if the Inspector got on, you'd quickly issue them with a cheap ticket so he wouldn't know. She used to work at the same depot as my dad.

'He was just like a film star,' she says. 'The best-looking man I'd ever seen.' She made sure she worked the same shifts as he did, then managed to get assigned to the same bus and then sat with him in the canteen and then became his friend. She must have worn him down.

Cold, damp wind buffets down the aisle of the bus and right past my bare legs and up my skirt. I don't have a winter coat yet, just my school blazer and a thin white shirt and my Waverley tie.

I get off at Camp Hill and have to cross the busy dual carriageway to catch the next bus, the number 16 or 17, that takes me to Small Heath. Dad told me to always walk to the crossing, but it's a hundred yards away and I'm so tired. If the traffic lights are on red, all the traffic has to stop right by the junction and I can just nip over the two lanes, duck under the flyover and do the same on the other side. I can save yards and minutes and a hundred shivers in the cold and wet.

I wait at the edge of the pavement. Cars rush past, lorries thunder by and I stand back so I don't get splashed, watching the lights change from green to amber, then red. But there's hardly a gap before the next load of cars come and I have to run really quickly. I see a white van and I dash past it just in time.

I am a foot from safety when the pale-green Anglia hits me. I knew I was too slow. Out of the corner of my eye, with a somersault heart, I see it following the curve of the road. I see it come alongside the white van, then overtake it. It's too close. I pull my satchel to my chest like it might save me. I watch my PE bag drop under the wheel and then I'm light as a feather, spinning up and losing everything and worrying in that airborne instant, will I be late, will my pumps get run over, will everything get wet in the rain?

I come down on my right side, hard, and scuff my forehead on the dirty concrete under the flyover. I hear the van brake and the cars stop and car doors open. And car doors slam. But all I see is the dust and rubbish on the ground under the flyover and think that at least I am dry lying under here and maybe after all I won't get told off for having wet hair and a muddy skirt and maybe someone will look after my pumps.

'Don't move her!' a man shouts.

I close my eyes and try to turn my head but I can't. I am crying and a woman says, 'Shhhh. The ambulance is coming.'

'I didn't see her. I didn't see her. I didn't see her.'

He sounds so young. There are other men telling him it's not his fault and I want to nod and agree, but my neck hurts and one of my legs feels like it's not there. Over all of it, over everything, my hip is thudding and I want to turn my body over and get my weight off it.

'Don't move,' says the woman.

'The crossing's right there,' says someone else.

'I didn't see her,' he says again.

I'm sitting up in bed on the children's ward when Mom comes. I can see she's been crying as well. She's wearing a false smile for the nurse, but her face is red and she's bunching her hands together.

When I got to the hospital, they asked me what my phone number was, but we don't have a phone so I had to tell them the name and address of Mr and Mrs Byrne because they do have a phone, and they looked up the number of Byrnes in the phone book and Mr Byrne would have run round to tell Mom because he's good like that, in an emergency. Once, when I got lost after hockey, I did the same thing, only that time I had to ring 100 and talk to the operator and she put me straight through to Mr Byrne and he went and got Mom and then they both came to collect me from the wrong side of Hockley. Dad told me off when I got home. He said I'd taken the wrong bus and that I had to pay more attention to what I was doing, but I hadn't been at Waverley Grammar School very long then and didn't know the way home.

I'm so glad to see Mom that I try to smile but it comes out wrong and I'm crying again. I've got a plaster on my forehead and a bandage on my arm. I'm only wearing my vest and knickers and even though I'm under a blanket

I feel cold and one of my legs keeps moving. The other leg is the one that got hurt, the one that the nurse wiped with stinging ointment and covered over with something that looks like a square nappy.

'We don't think she needs an X-ray,' says the nurse, patting Mom and not me. 'She only got clipped by the car, fortunately. He must have braked just in time. She landed on her right side, but she's mobile and nothing's broken. Very lucky girl. We'll keep her in – bang on the head, can't be too careful.'

Mom's nodding and trying to look like she'd say 'Kids, eh?' if she could find her voice, but all she can do is swallow and blink and hold my hand while the nurse talks to her. She's squeezing my hand too hard.

The nurse moves close in to Mom and drops her voice. 'He's outside,' she says, 'the young man who hit her. We had to give him something for the shock. Pale as death, he was. Poor thing. He said he wouldn't leave until he'd spoken to you.'

I start crying harder now because I know what Mom's like when someone does something to one of us. Once, I was walking home from the rec with Tracey and Dean. It was the end of the day, the sun was turning thick and milky, and I saw, just by a garden wall, a small blue flower with a yellow stripe. It was nodding its head, tired like we were, but it was bright, bright blue and so pretty it made me stop. I bent over, broke the stem and picked it.

'Oi!' A man marched out of the house and pointed at me. 'I saw that!'

I dropped the flower and grabbed Dean's hand.

'It was falling over,' I said.

'You people!' he said. 'Stealing, that's what it is! Dirty little thief.'

He picked up the flower and pushed me backwards and bent over, inches from my face.

'Go on! Get back to where you came from!'

I put my head down and we walked home. Mom saw my face when I opened the front door.

'What?' she said. I start telling her about the blue flower and the man who shoved me and before I finish she's marching up Springfield Road in her overall, chewing her tongue as she goes.

'Come on!' she shouts as she swings her arm and digs her heels into the pavement. I hurry after her. The man is still outside when she gets there. Two of his neighbours are outside, all folded arms and heads held stiffly, while he tells them about the immigrant thief.

Mom is on him like a beast. 'Who do you think you are? Did you put your hands on my child?'

He holds the flower up like it will protect him. It's wilted and sad-looking in his fat, white paw.

'She picked this out of my garden,' he says, but he's shaken, wearing a different face from the one that sprayed his spittle on my cheek.

'Show me,' said my mother.

He points to a corner where his garden wall ends and the path meets the pavement. It's a square inch of no man's land, neither his private garden nor the public street.

Mom pushes her face up towards him and jabs her finger in his chest.

'Don't you *ever* touch one of my children again!' she hisses. He leans away from her. The neighbours hurry inside, away from the mad Irishwoman with the hard jaw and fearless finger. 'And wait till my husband hears about this!' she throws behind her.

She grabs my hand and marches home again.

'Ha!' she says. 'That'll give him nightmares.'

But we both know she won't tell Dad and if she did he'd only shake his head and say, 'You can't trust the white man,' and that would be that.

Now, here she was again, about to lay into someone who had hurt one of her kids, except this time it's different.

I keep pulling her hand until she looks away from the nurse. 'It was my fault, Mom. Don't tell him off.'

But the nurse takes Mom away and I have to wait ages until she comes back.

'What a lovely boy,' she says. 'He's had a such a shock. He looks terrible.' She's smiling properly now, pleased that the boy has somehow got his undeserved comeuppance.

The nurse brings all the children ice cream on a trolley, but I'm not hungry. Mom tells me to eat up while she spends ages going round the ward talking to all the other children and their moms.

She's got her voice back now, 'confident mother' voice, unfazed. 'No, you wouldn't believe it, would you?' she says to one woman. 'Car accident. She was trying not to be late for school. We've told her a hundred times. Kids, eh?'

Eventually, she gives me a kiss and goes home. The nurse puts a clever table over my bed and hands me a colouring book and some pencils. She says I can't go to sleep and I have to have a wee as soon as I can. Every time she walks past my bed, she gives me loads of orange squash and biscuits, and then helps me shuffle to the toilet. She waits outside to listen and then takes me back to bed. My hip really hurts and I'm very tired, but she keeps telling me to colour in or read a book or talk to the other children and it's not time for sleeping, not for hours yet. She's got no idea that I've been up all night watching the lights on the ceiling and waiting for Dad to go to work.

The next morning, Mom comes back with different clothes for me to put on. My uniform is all dirty and covered in blood so she puts it in her bag and helps me hobble outside. And there, waiting for us, is Dad. He's come to get me in the car. Only then do I realize how serious it all is. He doesn't get out, but he watches Mom help me over the road and then he leans behind him and opens the door so I can get in.

'What I tell you?' he says.

'I didn't see the car,' I answer.

'It see you, though, ain't it?'

I cry quietly in case I make him angry. Mom tells him what the nurse said.

'We've got to keep an eye on her, Arthur, and if anything changes we have to bring her back in.'

'I tired tell these children,' he says as he drives away. 'Tired.'

In a few days I'm well enough to go back to school. I show Kate and Anne the bruises on my legs and arms and I don't have to do PE for weeks. Miss Brown, the PE teacher with the husky voice and downy blond cheeks, tells me that I can go and sit in the library or help her take the equipment out on to the field. I choose the library, but I don't read the books, I stare and stare out of the window. I make shapes out of the clouds, I watch raindrops chase each other down the glass, I colour in every 'o' and 'p', 'd' and 'q' in my Geography textbook. I do everything except read. I have to read in English, I have to read Jehovah's Witness books at the meeting on Sunday, on Tuesday, on Thursday. I have to read the Bible. I will not read if I don't have to. Instead, I luxuriate in the nothingness, the free roam of my tired mind, the pure unfettered drift of my thoughts like wisps of summer clouds in a pale-blue sky.

There are six black children in the whole school. Me and Kim are two of them. I'm nearly two years younger and yet I follow her only a year behind and applaud her on to the stage when she gets the School Award for Art, the School Award for Music, some prize or other for the discus and special mentions on Speech Day at the end of the year for some certificate, some good girl's prize. She's a child who chats to the teachers without going red in the face and gets the swot's pass to the staffroom at lunchtime.

Some mornings, if we want a change from the numbers 91 and 17, we get the number 1 bus to school, but it means, inevitably, that we will probably meet the English teacher with the round glasses, deep voice. Kim likes him. He likes Kim. She sits, out of choice, next to him on the top deck so they can point out the Victorian chimneys and then talk about poetry. She uses words she doesn't use with me.

She talks about things I don't understand that she keeps for other people. The same teacher gives me lines because I can't spell 'character'.

I'm clever and near the top in nearly every lesson, but I don't do more than the minimum, even in English. I'm too scared to race ahead in *Great Expectations* or *The Merchant of Venice* because it will mean I will know the plot before the class gets to the end of the book, which in turns means deeper levels of boredom and desperation for the lesson to be over.

I memorize whole passages of *The Merchant of Venice* and feel sympathy only for Shylock, for him against the world and the posh people who have stitched him up.

'Do we not bleed?' I say to myself and understand his exacting nature.

And I love the way Joe Gargery speaks to Pip. 'What larks!' I say under my breath, rolling the 'r'.

I picture the hulking blacksmith in his little forge, berated by the harridan Mrs Joe, his kind eyes and his big heart ever open to the boy who makes good. I sink into the Kentish marshes and watch for convicts. I shudder in graveyards and make crumpets in my gentleman's rooms in Gray's Inn.

And then I come to and find myself on the second floor of Waverley Grammar School, on the east side of Birmingham, in the middle of a long winter's afternoon, and the class will hardly have moved on.

'Now, Queenan. Top of page 41. To the next two paragraphs.'

We proceed at a snail's pace, ripping the heart out of Miss Havisham all over again.

Mathematics starts off OK in the first year but, eventually, Mrs Allen introduces letters. She's a tiny Welsh woman with a tight, wavy hairdo in stripes of black and grey. She always wears a nice cardigan in an all-over diamond pattern. She has lots of them in different pastel colours. She never shouts but everyone is always quiet in her lessons. Even Queenan, who isn't quiet for anyone. He's the only boy in the class who looks like he should shave.

Mrs Allen walks to the blackboard and starts writing.

I look around the class expecting to meet bewildered faces or horror or giggles. What's going on?

'What is x?' she asks.

I think this is a trick question involving the apples of Derek and Barbara's pears, but Mrs Allen is smiling.

'Algebra,' she announces in the same voice that a normal person would say 'Doughnuts'.

'Now, children, x is unknown.'

I agree.

'And b is unknown.'

Correct.

'So, let's start with x.'

I watch her mouth move and her white chalky hand scratch on the blackboard, more and more letters, and now brackets and now different letters, until y somehow appears.

And right there, right at that moment, I unplug. I feel the whole of algebra and my fingertip grasp of long division slip forever into a filing cabinet marked 'Who cares?', where it will meet the chemical symbol for boron, the size of a frog's heart and the name of the man who invented the heat exchanger. Where's the story in random facts? Where's the story in algebra? What's it for? When will I ever need it? Tell me about the princess and the frog, tell me about the childhood of Mr Heat Exchanger or his wife or his broken arm, and I can plug in again.

It's the same in other subjects that involve remembering facts. I sit near the front in Geography and copy down everything the teacher says, neat, endless pages of beautiful handwriting that keep me awake, the only way to pay attention, their meaning and application vaguely understood. And then, at the end of the year, I regurgitate everything for the exams. I always choose to be the person who writes things down for experiments in Biology and Chemistry, grabbing the pen and exercise book before anyone can object. I muddle through and fly under the radar until algebra finds me out. It is lost to me and yet it feels like no loss at all.

By the time I am fifteen I am in the lowest Maths class with Mr Venus, whose speciality is crowd control, distraction and nose-picking. He leaves us alone, the naughty boys, dyscalculic girls and dunces, sets us little jobs of copying down fractions hoping something will stick through sheer repetition.

The whole school takes O levels except for Venus's CSE class of Maths misfits. I sit and face pages of multiple-choice questions that I don't bother to read and, at the end of it all, I am graced with a Grade 4 award, no doubt

for my neatness and lovely handwriting. I'm shocked to
have anything.

Mom always goes to Parents' Evening alone. Dad says he's
working. She puts on her best coat and carries a handbag.
We have to wait at home.

When she comes back, she has my report and stands
in the door of the telly room to tell Dad what the teachers
said.

'You wouldn't think it was Mandy's Parents' Evening,
Arthur. It was Kim this and Kim that. They hardly talked
about Mandy. She's top in everything.'

'Who?' says Dad.

'Kim.'

'What them say?'

'The English teacher said she writes lovely poems and
she's brilliant at Biology. But Art is her best subject.'

'Mandy?'

'No, Arthur. Kim.'

It's a relief that they end up where they always do, talking about Kim's cleverness, while I dissolve, invisible, and
don't have to answer their questions or talk about what
I've learned or what I know or what I want to be when I
grow up. I drift upstairs and leave Mom talking to the side
of my dad's face while he watches *News at Ten*.

19

The Irish are Like That

At Waverley Grammar School we have Music once a week, but in the autumn half-term they bump this up to three. Christmas approaches. We are learning the 'Hallelujah' chorus for the Christmas Concert.

The music room is near the assembly hall, a massive room with a high ceiling and wooden floor, thirty chairs circling a grand piano. There's no blackboard, no desks, just light and space and the feeling, as you walk through the door, that some part of you might be brought alive by the music. You might learn the opening chorus of the operetta *Robin Hood* or be one of the 'three little maids' of *The Mikado* with Mr Martin bouncing up and down on his spongy Nature Trek shoes, poking his baton at 'You!' now 'You!', and your heart swells and you rise to it and sing with your chest out, curling your tongue around 'The Modern Major-General'. 'And again!' Mr Martin shouts as we near the end. 'And again!'

I wait by Mr Martin's desk at the front of the music room. The whole class is quiet. 'Yes?' he says.

'Mom says I can't learn any hymns, sir.'

Mr Martin frowns and smooths inches of lank red hair over the top of his bald head. He stands and adjusts his black gown, chalk-marked and creased, scruffier than every other teacher's.

'Hymns? Hymns?' he says, as though I've spoken a

foreign language. 'Does your mother believe in God?'
Everyone is listening.

'Yes, sir. We're Jehovah's Witnesses.'

'Listen,' he says and walks to the piano. He bangs his
fingers on the keys and bellows at full strength.

'"For the Lord God omnipotent reigneth!" Do you
believe that God is Lord?'

'Yes, sir, but—'

'And that the Lord is omnipotent, all-knowing, all-
seeing, and reigns over the heavens and the earth?'

'Yes, sir, but—'

'Then this is not a hymn, is it, girl? It is a statement of
fact. Tell your mother you are announcing statements of
facts set to music. Go and sit down. You are not excused.'

Oh, the beauty of it. The sweet release. I am not excused.
There's nothing I can do about it. He passes round sheets
of music and goes to each child.

'*For the Lord God omnipotent reigneth!* Sing it, boy! . . .
Tenor. Next! You, yes, you,' he says to Queenan, the only
boy who's shaving. 'The same. Sing!'

He listens with his eyes closed. 'Bass. Good. At least
we'll have one. Next!'

And so it goes until, after a short solo, he decides I will
sing alto.

Hallelujah! Hallelujah! Hallelujah! Hallelujah!
   Hallelujah!

I learn my part, practise my part, guard it in my heart.
Kim, a soprano, has had the same talk from Mr Martin, that
we are singing Handel's statement of fact that God shall

reign forever and ever, accompanied by a little orchestral support, and we sing in harmony at the bus stop, on our walks home, in bed when the others are asleep. We sing until we are perfect, until Mr Martin has Kim in the front row, soprano, and me right behind her, and the concert is set for a Tuesday night. A Tuesday night. Meeting night. A Christmas concert.

After rehearsals one day, we are on the first of the three buses we take from school to home.

'She won't come, will she?' I ask Kim about Mom because Kim knows how she thinks.

'She might.'

'We could tell her it was just a play or something, or just a rehearsal for something.'

That's the other thing about Kim, she won't lie. She says nothing. She wants this as much as I do. It's a whole-school concert and she's in the front row. She could have been in the orchestra with her violin, but her voice is so pure and piercing that she's right in front of Mr Martin, and when he digs the baton in the air, he digs it straight at her with joy.

'What shall we say?' I ask.

Later that same night, we are walking home from the bus stop after a house meeting. It's late. We are cold, we are tired. As usual, Mom's talking to Kim about what we've learned.

'Isn't it interesting that the Greeks have so many words for "love"?' she says, holding Karen's hand and looking up at Kim for instruction, as usual overawed by Kim's intelligence and grasp of complex doctrine. She asks Kim about stars, maths, kings, prophecies, dynasties, dinosaurs, poets, painters, and Kim always has an answer, delivered with the authority of the old and wise.

'Yes, Brother Christou said there were seven,' she answers, 'but *agapé* is the love Jehovah has for us.'

Tracey, Dean and I, by wordless agreement, slow down, hang back, careful not to get drawn into yet more religious instruction after two endless hours of it.

Kim continues. 'We should take every opportunity to praise him, shouldn't we?'

'Yes,' says Mom, assuming the role of pupil.

'We're learning about it at school. Something written in the eighteenth century, about the role of public praise in worship.'

My ears prick up. She couldn't be so clever, could she?

Mom has her head bowed. She sniffs. 'I wish I'd been good at school. I was too busy looking after my brothers and sisters and I never got the chance to—'

Kim is not so easily distracted and, anyway, we've heard this lament a thousand times. 'It was written by someone called Handel.'

'Handel,' repeats my mother, hoping it will bed down in her underused brain.

'It's very interesting, actually.' Kim half turns so I can glean her intent. 'And we're going to a concert about it the week after next.'

'About what?'

'The importance of public worship, Mom. Exactly what we were learning about at the meeting. The necessity of having a response to *agapé* and its role in our service as

Christians. The omniscience of the creator, Hebrews, chapter 1, verse 8. Christ's reign over all the earth as in Luke, chapter 1, verse 33.'

One too many concepts for the uneducated Irish girl from the misty green fields of Wexford. Mom falls to silence.

'It's the first week in December, a Tuesday,' Kim pursues. 'Me and Mandy will be going.'

'OK, love.'

I'm on the bus to school the next day and realize something has changed. The conductor is talking to everyone about the bomb and all the buses are being diverted away from town. There are traffic jams everywhere and a scary sort of feeling in the air.

By the time I get to class the register has already been taken and I have to explain to the teacher why I'm late.

'You live in Moseley, don't you?' says Mr Ellis.

'Yes, sir.'

'Did you come through town?'

'Digbeth, sir, so yes, nearly.'

'Right, OK. Sit down.'

Everyone looks at me. I haven't been told off and don't know why. We have to go straight to a special assembly.

Mr Mills stands and there is an immediate hush.

'Children,' he says, 'many of you will already know that there was a bomb in the city centre last night.'

Murmuring and shuffling.

'Quiet! As far as we are aware, no member of staff nor any pupils of this school are missing nor were in any

KIT DE WAAL

way involved. Nevertheless, we are aware that this is an extremely distressing event. Many young people lost their lives last night and no doubt there are many more fatalities yet to come.'

All the teachers are on the stage behind the Head-master. They look shocked and pale. Mrs Heatherington looks like she might cry.

'We will say a prayer.'

I do not move. I won't walk out while the whole school watches and not be part of this, so I put my head down and see Kim do the same.

By lunchtime the news is everywhere. It's the IRA. There are huddles of children talking about what they know and who might have died and how their cousin nearly went to that pub and their dad knows someone who knows some-one who could have died but didn't.

One girl crosses her arms and screws up her face. 'My mom says the Irish are like that. They just want to kill us all. They're murderers and they don't care who they hurt.'

'Yes,' says another, 'the bombers will be hiding in a dirty Irish house right now, but the police will get them. I mean, Irish people are so thick and stupid they'll get caught.'

I stand and listen then walk away but all week it's the same. Every day someone else dies and the IRA are con-demned by someone new. Every day there's a victim's mother or brother or sister or son interviewed on telly or in the newspaper and every day the Irish are worse than the day before – terrorists, murderers, evil, stupid. No one

166

knows I'm Irish. I'm the black girl at school and unless I stand up and declare my Irishness no one will ever guess. I say nothing.

One night there's a knock at the door. It's the police.

'We're looking for Mr O'Loughlin,' they say. Dad gets up and joins Mom on the front doorstep.

'Mr O'Loughlin?' says the copper.

'Yes,' says Dad. 'What's it about?'

'You're Mr O'Loughlin?'

'Yes, that's me.'

'Oh!' says the copper 'We're looking for someone . . . else.'

The other copper steps in. 'It's about the bombs, sir,' he says, 'sorry to trouble you, just following up on a lead. Not to worry. Enjoy your evening, sir.'

We watch them leave, disappointed not to see a panda car parked outside the house.

'They should have talked to you, eh, Sheilo?' says Dad, but Mom's face is like thunder.

'That's not funny, Arthur. No Irish person can hold their head up in Birmingham any more. Don't joke about it.'

And so the concert comes and goes. We stay after school that Tuesday with no packed tea like the other children bring. We have no extra money to go to the shop under special dispensation to get sweets, but we are used to the hunger.

The hall fills up with parents. Neither one of ours. We sing and we are applauded and afterwards the Headmaster smiles and says, 'Very good, both of you.'

We manage to get two biscuits each from the plates that are set out for the adults and as we nibble them on the number 17 bus we relive our moment in the spotlight, the crowds of teachers and parents, the sweet harmonies and soaring chorus. Hallelujah.

20

The Men are Coming!

The house smells of hot iron and Bay Rum.

'Sheilo! Sheilo!' Dad calls from their bedroom.

Dad's getting dressed and this is an event. He has been up since morning choosing and discarding suit after suit, the blue mohair or the black wool, shoe after shoe, the Chelsea boots or the black brogues, matching handker-chiefs and ties, a pale-blue shirt, no, a white one, no again, a light grey.

Mom smooths a scalding iron on brown paper covering yards of the navy mohair that has been made by hand into my father's three-piece suit, shades of blue and black and green like a peacock feather. I carry his shirt, his vest, his socks and underpants upstairs in a holy pile and the bedroom door opens a crack, his mighty hand grabs the bundle and it closes again. Then I run downstairs for my next task. The front room must sparkle. The men are coming.

As she presses Dad's waistcoat, Mom doles out jobs like an overseer. Kim polishes Dad's shoes, swirling black wax into box-fresh Chelsea boots and polishing it off again with a yellow duster. I pour KP Nuts into never-used glass bowls and place them on the glass coffee table in the middle of the front room. Never-used cushions on never-used chairs are smoothed and plumped while never-used carpet is vacuumed and the waxed radiogram is loaded up with Nat King Cole and Jim Reeves. The window is opened a crack and I dance around with air freshener and Johnson's polish. The men are coming.

We must dress up for the thirty seconds they will see us. Mom wears a yellow dress with big green roses on the skirt. She scrapes her hair into a savage bun and puts sandals on her little feet. She knows these men from her first days with Dad. The men who didn't go with white women, who married the women they brought over, the glossy black women with proper hairdos and cookery skills. She feels less than those women and her memories force her lips into a thin straight line that some people might think is a smile.

She tells us stories about the men when Dad is out.

'Judas didn't get a name like that for nothing. And Stump? All smiles now but not when I knew him. Grumble couldn't stand me and the feeling was mutual.'

She sends Dean to stand outside on the front-garden wall to wait for them, to wave them to the right house. To give her a few minutes' warning. It's Christmas or some independence day, it's someone's birthday, the cricket is on, someone won something or someone's died. That's when the men come and Dad is transformed.

'Stump!'

'Judas!'

'Sugar!'

'Harry!'

'Grumble!'

'George!'

Dad never hurries. He slouches downstairs with his easy walk and immaculate self. He wears a big gold watch and a short-sleeved shirt with too many pockets. He stops at the bottom of the stairs and looks in the hallway mirror. His licks a finger and smooths it over his eyebrows, he adjusts everything and nothing. His swagger is a front. We know without being told that he's nervous, this man who hardly drinks, who never parties, who goes nowhere, only to Leeds once a year for the carnival, only to the bus depot on a Thursday night, only to the Sunset Cinema Club in town and rarely. These are the men from home, from his childhood games, from the boat and his first days in England. Made-good men.

We hover around the front door and clutter the narrow hallway as they come, blocking out the light, shaking hands and easing past one another into the best room at the front of the house. The noise thrills, the accents, the foreign joviality, the sense of something exciting and normal and knowing that for a moment we are like everyone else, like people who have visitors and parties and nuts in bowls.

'Lord! Look Tracey! She big, eh? How big you is, Tracey?'

'No, no, Sugar! You mad? This is Kim, isn't it? Kim?'

One big hand holds my head, pivots it side to side, touches my hair, strokes it, long and wavy. I'm examined for my skinniness and my Indian looks.

'And this is Mandy! She meagre, eh? She look like a cha-cha man child, don't it?'

My mother hates this. Tries her best to smile at the long-running joke. My mother, who presents her virtue as a single slip with the man she later married, is quick to take offence and put an ocean between herself and the other kind of white women who went with black men in the fifties and sixties, easy, loose, drinkers, prostitutes, low class. But it's too late for that. The joke persists.

'You sure this one is yours, Lofty?' says Sugar, cuffing me under the chin, turning my head so everyone can see my long, straight plaits.

My father laughs as I try to stand behind him. 'You don't see the gap in her teeth, Sugar? You remember mine? Me no worry.'

Dean and Karen weave between the legs of the visitors like hungry cats. The boy is noticed, the baby isn't. Dean might get a pass into the front room but we girls won't.

Sugar is slight with wavy black hair and a thin moustache. George is tall, like someone from a film, something regal about him, my father's best friend. It's Stump I like best. He has a wide smile and a goatee beard that bobs up and down when he laughs, and he's always laughing. He's short and wide, wears his belt and trousers up high and he has a gold tooth on one side that glints in the light from his eyes. He's the one who always notices my mother when the others don't.

'Sheila,' he says, 'you good?' He claps his hands. He smells of man and thyme and the back-home I have never seen.

And Harry comes in last. Pale and delicate, never filling out his light-grey suit, a round balding head, Chinese with a West Indian accent so strong it's hard to understand. He drinks rum like water and we mimic his 'ki ki ki' laugh for weeks after he's left.

When the door closes, we wait outside in the fragrant space they've left behind. It's all muffled in the front room and what we can hear we barely understand. There are long sentences in Kittian patois, there are long run-ups to the jokes, there are interjections and the rumble of Stump's deep voice and then *BOOM!* The laughter of a hundred voices, bass tone waves crash and roll and roll again in the retelling and expansion, in the falling-away and aftermath.

So goes the afternoon and into the evening, but they never stay late. These men were really going somewhere else but they have stopped off to see their friend, the one who never goes out, the one who keeps himself apart, not a drinker, hardly a gambler, not a womanizer or a dancer. If they want to see Lofty, they have to come to him, so they do, for old times' sake, for the memories he has of home. Now, the goodbyes are long in the making, a huddle up by the front door and a last joke, the draining of glasses and waving and waving until the cars pull away and the house is dead again. They leave their scent and the smell of rum and whisky, they leave a faint taste of a boyhood life elsewhere, heat and sand and everlasting blue skies, they leave crumbs on the carpet and the feeling in my belly that my life could be different, that Stump's children are lucky.

Dad never leaves with them but that evening, perhaps because he's dressed and because maybe he's had a tot of rum and he's lonely for the sound of patois and jokes that have been running since 1952, and because maybe there's a little bit of regret that he said no, again, always says no when they ask him to come with them, and because some days he wishes he was one of the boys, making a little shuffle-step to the calypso, to the steel pan, and sometimes the sunless country and the relentless white man gets him down, sometimes he wants the taste of yearning rinsed away, so that evening he goes down to the bus depot for a game of cards.

He hefts on his overcoat and settles his trilby just so. He puts his face to the mirror, stands back a little, checks himself over. This is no cursory glance. The hat is adjusted to the millimetre. A little clothes brush is kept up by the front door for just this moment. He takes it or I take it or one of the others and he's brushed down. We can't reach his shoulders but we can swipe at invisible dust on his back and his hem.

'It's done, Dad.'

We run to the kitchen for a cloth for his shoes that have to shine, shine, shine. Then, a last neck stretch. A lean into the mirror. A close-up. A practice of his wide smile. Ah, yes. There he is.

'Good,' he says and packs paragraphs into that word. 'Looking fine, Arthur boy. Yes, you lookin' all right. You still can wear a coat. You need to look right when people see you, don't it, Arthur? Yes, so don't cut no corners. You see Sugar's Chelsea boots? Them was a nice boot. Must get me some like that. And George and Stump and Sugar, they all come to your house, Arthur, and see your nice clothes and if people ask "How was Lofty?" they can't say nothing bad. The children behave. Sheila smiled and I spend plenty money on food and drink. Things is expensive but is only once a year, ain't it, Arthur boy? You got to make sure everything is just so. Make the children brush you down, that's what children is for. All right, now we is talkin'.'

'Good,' he says again. I watch him go to the front door.

'Sheilo?' he calls but doesn't wait for an answer. 'I going out to come back.'

He never takes her with him. Never tells her to get a frock on, 'We going dancing, Sheilo!' Never sticks his elbow out for her, never holds her coat. In all my life, they never leave the house together and stroll down Springfield Road arm in arm. They leave at separate times, for separate things, to separate places. He closes the front door and the house settles under his absence. Wherever we are in the house, we know that he has left, that the telly room is ours, that we can sit on the radiator and relax. Dad is out. And there are crisps and nuts in the front room.

21

Beautiful Dreamer

It is my birthday. I am fourteen. I wake up and tell Tracey.

'Happy Birthday,' she whispers. She can say nothing more and I can't mention it to anyone else. Dean is only ten and might blurt something out and Karen is seven and too naive for secrets. Kim would disapprove of the concept, so all I can do is whisper it to Tracey who can whisper it back. Then the celebrations are done. The closest I can come to imagining birthday presents is by playing the new game we've invented.

As well as childminding and a bit of cleaning, Mom has started running catalogues for the neighbours, big fat catalogues full of clothes and shoes and toys and furniture, kettles and cutlery, garden tools and blankets. We get out the Great Universal catalogue. Or Littlewoods. Or Grattan. We put it on the kitchen table. Two of us, sometimes three of us, sit around it and one is in charge of turning the pages. We go straight to the toy section. Whoever turns the page has a disadvantage but that's just the way it is. Right. Turn the page. Then, as quick as you can, you have to put your finger on the toy that you want the most and the others have to have what's left. That toy is yours, nobody else's, except if it's your birthday and then you have first claim but only for that day. We linger on each page and imagine what it would be like to have an Etch A Sketch or KerPlunk. On the Meccano and Lego pages everyone gets something really good, but there are pages and pages of dolls which can get boring so sometimes we move on to the kitchen pages. We buy food mixers and saucepan sets, matching plates and different cookers. We buy colourful plastic beakers and picnic baskets, carpet sweepers in two different colours and washing-up bowls that match the plate drainers. Sometimes we go to the bra pages and choose matching underwear and panty girdles or choose stuff for Mom that we know she can't afford.

Dad comes in while we're playing. He stands at the door of the kitchen and looks different. He has a surprised look on his face, a happy look, proud and excited at the same time.

'Come look,' he says.

We follow him out to the front of the house. He's standing by a massive car in silver and navy blue, the best car I have ever seen. And where is our old car?

'Princess 3 litre, Vanden Plas. You know what Vanden Plas means?'

'No, Dad.'

'Look inside. Get in.'

We slide into the back seat and he points it all out to us: the little walnut tables that fold out of the leather like magic; the chrome ashtray with a special button that makes the ash vanish; armrests that disappear back from whence they came; and more strips of walnut, everywhere as posh as anything we've ever seen.

'That is Vanden Plas,' he says, saying the words slowly and clearly like he learned them an hour ago. 'All them little things there, all that interior style. You can't beat Vanden Plas.'

No one else has a car like ours, there's nothing to touch it on the street. It's the only car that suits my father when he's dressed up or when he's going to the depot for a game of cards. It's the only car that's big enough for him, wide enough for him. I hope the neighbours are looking or someone I know comes past.

Mom stands on the front step.

'You bought a new car, Arthur?' she says.

'Look good, don't it?' he answers. 'Come, we go for a spin.'

She looks at him in his good suit and his good shoes with neat waves in his black hair, his tall and immaculate self, proud and excited and asking her for once in her life to go out with him for a little drive, and she turns and goes inside. She sits at the kitchen table and starts adding up the catalogue money she's been collecting for weeks, noting down numbers and names and dates with a yellow plastic biro in her still-foreign right hand, making additions on a scrap of paper to keep the totals neat. It always ends the same way. She starts muttering to herself, starts talking aloud.

'That makes six, that makes nineteen and that makes . . . no, wait. Peggy's already paid. I haven't got enough, then . . . no, wait . . .' And so it goes until the tears come and she asks one of us to help. It is never me.

Eventually, she folds the notes and puts the coins in an envelope. She sighs loud and long.

'A new car. There's me working all hours God sends and handing my money over so he can buy a new car. You're a bloody idiot, Sheila.'

The next week, Mom buys herself a harmonica. She buys herself a Davy Crockett-style fur hat. Every day, she sits on the back step wearing her hat in the shade and learning the harmonica with her eyes closed.

She cups the harmonica at each end and draws it smoothly backwards and forwards and then jerks it at the end to make it warble. Over and over she goes, breathing in and out so there are no gaps in the tune, and every so often, when she loses her way, she drops it away from her mouth and hums or sings under her breath to remind herself of the notes. '*Beautiful dreamer, wake unto me . . .*'

No matter where we are, whether we have climbed over the fence at the end of the garden and into the school playing fields to make castles in the sandpit at the end of the long jump, whether we are lying on the corrugated-tin roof sunning ourselves and running marbles down the grooves, whether we are playing records in the front room while we tidy it or sitting out the front watching people walk past, wherever we are, we can hear her harmonica. The jobs are left undone, the house is even more chaotic than usual.

She walks us up Woodlands Road to the house meeting in Moseley Village, on Cotton Lane, the Davy Crockett hat on the back of her head, two long brown plaits under the furry hat's tail as she plays a simple marching song on her harmonica. The posh people watch us walk past their gates, a ragtag confederacy of underdressed black children trailing reluctantly after their mad mother. Just before she gets to the big Victorian house where the meeting is, she tucks the harmonica in her bag with her Bible and *Babylon the Great* study book. She slips her hat off before she can be seen by the truly holy Jehovah's Witnesses with their normal English ways.

When it's ended and we are walking home again, when the street lights have come on and it's almost dark, out comes the hat and she rallies us for another forty-minute walk, singing a verse then playing a verse, and we join in. Sometimes it's a ballad from an old film, sometimes, when we're tired, a marching song that keeps our legs moving ever onwards towards home.

It's not so bad when there's no one around and we're all together. We don't care then if our mother looks crazy and lives out the life she wished she had in a hippy, free-love commune on the West Coast of America, as a rugged lumberjack's wife in the Outback of Australia, as a pioneer in the wilds of Canada, building her own house with her own two hands and raising a flock of obedient children.

We walk home to the plaintive off-kilter tune of the lone warbler sitting on a rickety porch somewhere in the Adirondack Mountains, calling across the valley, the wood chopped and crackling under an iron range, two Palomino ponies nibbling prairie grass and a sturdy woman in a Davy Crockett hat, a check shirt and old denim jeans playing for the crickets and friendly Sioux.

We know that's where she's gone and there's no calling

her back until she's good and ready, not Jehovah, not my father, not her children. Anywhere but here with us is where she wants to be.

Every year or so, the times of the Sunday meetings rotate so that the other congregation who use the Kingdom Hall can have the afternoon slot and we have a twelve-month taste of misery, getting up early on Sundays in the dead of winter to walk, tired, cold and hungry, to the bus stop on Stratford Road, getting off early to save money and walking some more with needles of slanting rain on our bare legs to the Kingdom Hall to worship the almighty, ever-merciful and loving God of All Things.

It's half past eight on a Sunday morning. To stimulate our devotion, Mom selects one of her Country and Western records and puts it on full blast. We have Irish neighbours either side who are probably at Mass themselves and who are, in any event, ethnically bonded to Val Doonican and Conway Twitty and their tales of love's frustration and grinding rural poverty.

At least some of the Country and Western women, with their enormous bouffants and over-plucked eyebrows, look like they might have had the odd boyfriend and sexual experience. They warble on about affairs, honky-tonks and fights over men and a six-dollar dress. I wander down to the kitchen, fully dressed and seething with disobedience. I attempt to sit down.

'No, you don't,' says Mom, pushing me towards the door. 'Wake Kim up and find Karen some clothes.'

Back upstairs I go.

'Kim! Kim! Kim!' I have to throw the blankets off her and put my mouth three inches from her ear.

'Mom said get up!' She barely responds.

I sort through the four outfits that Karen has and choose a check dress and some white socks, a pair of knickers that look clean.

'Here,' I say, throwing them on her bed. 'Get up.'

Downstairs, Jim Reeves, with his clean-cut, close-shaved, antiseptic face, is on track five, 'Welcome to My World'. I know every word. Any minute now Mom will flip his greatest hits over and we'll be treated to 'He'll Have to Go' and 'Distant Drums'. Before I was fully awake, Jim was in bed with me, bellowing his country twang under the blanket and between the sheets. I cultivate a special hatred for Jim Reeves who has the latent menace of a high-ranking Jehovah's Witness, with his wavy hair, tight collar and off-duty Aran jumper, casually leaning out of the record sleeve whispering wholesome exhortations.

I'm starting the next song in my mind before the first one has finished. Everywhere I go, school, the meeting and now at home, someone is trying to brainwash me, and I can't stand it. I don't want to be forever good and compliant. I don't want to do as I'm told and never swear, steal or kiss a boy. I don't want to try harder in Maths and help Mom tidy up. I don't want to believe everything I'm told and always give the right answers. I don't want to hate badness before I've even tasted it.

The meeting on Sunday is in two halves. The first half is an open invitation, an hour-long, syrupy sermon of plati-tudes and promises for the newly interested and soon-to-be-baptized. Faithful Witnesses who have spent weeks and weeks knocking doors and hours and hours in Bible study do their best to get people to come along and hear the Good News of the Kingdom first-hand. We know that we, the congregation, are Jehovah's best adverts, so we have to be dressed up and be on our best behaviour.

So Dexter, who's coming off drugs, or Mary, the prostitute who's had enough of low wages and black eyes, Gwen, the unhappy housewife who's sick of plumping cushions, Alex, the inquisitive student from Birmingham University who knows no one else in the city, and anyone else 'hungering and thirsting for righteousness' who likes the sound of a paradise earth free of disease and political shenanigans, trots along to the Kingdom Hall and sits with their brand-new Bible and open heart as we pray for their salvation.

We sit towards the back, all of us on one long, uncomfortable row with Mom blocking the exit. Some Brother drones on about the life everlasting with tons of wholesome food, loaves, fishes, permanently temperate weather, all of us employed in meaningful, manual labour, living lives of calm moderation in identikit American-style ranch houses, singing Kingdom Songs, wearing 1950s clothes with the dead eyes of the truly bored.

The second half of the meeting, when the new people have gone home to ponder the scriptures and breathe a sigh of relief, is a study of the *Watchtower* magazine, an in-depth examination of some aspect of organizational doctrine, an opportunity for the powers that be to tell us another way to be different to the rest of the world and have much less fun.

Sometimes, in hushed tones, we get reminded of the absolute sanctity of blood and that having a blood transfusion is a sin and anyone who needed one and refused would be doing a wonderful thing. The pregnant woman who died in childbirth? Well, she will be resurrected by Jehovah and have her babies in paradise. The man who had the chain-saw accident and lost his arms and his life when he said no to a stranger's blood in hospital? He'll be cutting down trees in a world free from lapses in attention when the New World comes. The boy that got run over and went to hospital where his parents had a fight with the doctors about him having a blood transfusion – and they won, yay! – what faith, what faith. So, we must all, on this very special point of doctrine, stay strong in the face of Satan's attacks. After all, no one wants to be disfellowshipped for a pint of blood, do they? Or for agreeing to have someone else's kidney or heart shoved inside you which is abhorrent to a loving God that gave you your own special organs with which to worship him. But we've heard this for years and years and we've become immune to these exhortations. We zone out until home time and make damn sure we look both ways when we cross the road.

This week it's sex. It could be exciting. It could be excruciating. It will be both. All eyes are down on the page. Me and Tracey scan for the juicy bits. There are no juicy bits. Not even an artist's impression or photograph. Pure text. The minister leading the meeting is up on the stage, Brother Kastellanos, a Greek elder, father of five, tall as a tree in miles of chocolate-brown mohair with tan shoes and slicked-back hair.

'Brother Fletcher will read for us today.'

Up stands the nervous Brother Fletcher, a chunky builder from Doncaster, a trainee elder, newly married and partaking of the flesh. He walks to the front, in a too-small suit, and reads the first paragraph into the standing microphone. It's always about context in the beginning, a scripture or two on why we're different from 'the world' and why this precious magazine contains the word of God dispensed in an unbroken line from heaven direct to Columbia Heights, Brooklyn, home of the Watchtower Bible and Tract Society, hub of holiness. Brother Fletcher sits down again and Brother Kastellanos continues.

'So, Paragraph 1, Question A, why is it important to heed God's warning about sexual impropriety?'

Hands fly up to answer. It's going to get tricky later on. If you have to take part, better get it over and done with early while the questions are general and not too embarrassing. This is a subject where your expertise can betray your sins.

'Sister Obuke?'

Someone passes the tall African woman the Roving Microphone. Sister Obuke is new and she's nervous. There are some people who radiate wholesomeness. Sister Obuke is one of them, humble, kind and eager to belong. It's her misfortune that the Witnesses found her before, say, the Women's Institute or the Avon Lady, but it's too late to back out now.

'Keep it short, Sister,' I think to myself. 'Don't try and be too clever.'

She has the good sense to simply read a scripture about God's eternal love.

'Thank you, Sister Obuke. Now, Question B, who created us with the desire to have wholesome and fulfilling
relationships?'

One for the kids. Mom elbows Dean in the ribs. He
pretends to be engrossed in Paul's epistle to the Ephesians.

'Jehovah!' shouts Annette Ford, a photofit Anne of
Green Gables so clean of spirit you want to strangle her
with her own pigtails.

And on we go, a whistle-stop tour of every dodgy sexual
encounter in the Bible, Ham *uncovering Jacob's nakedness*,
whatever that means, Pharoah's wife trying it on with
Joseph, Lot offering a baying mob his two virgin daughters
if they back off and leave the two visiting angels to have
their dinner in peace, on and on and on until Paragraph
14 gets into the dark meat. Sexual positions. Tracey nudges
me, a tiny, barely visible, smile starting in her eyes. Here
we go.

The long, draughty room drops an octave into thunder-
ing silence. Valiant Brother Kastellanos continues.

'Paragraph 14, Question A, what can we learn from the
Bible on this topic? Anyone?'

There's some shuffling and coughing. All heads are
bowed, turning the pages of Ephesians. Or is it Song of
Solomon? Hmm, let me see. There is nothing but the turn
of rice paper. Then a small, wavering hand goes up at the
front. Sister Leonard, seventy-eight, unmarried and of the
Most Holy class.

'Yes, Sister?'

There is a great hush. Sister Leonard clears her narrow

throat. 'Second Samuel 12.24 says a husband must *lie* with his wife and there are many other scriptures that speak of *lying* with one another. So when in congress married couples must be lying down on a bed.'

'That's right, Sister Leonard. Lying down on a bed. Horizontal. Prone. One man and one woman. Married. In bed. Lying down. Horizontal.'

Got it.

'And what else does the Bible say on this subject, Question C? Yes, Brother Warwick at the back.'

Brother Warwick, enthusiastic in all things, grabs the microphone and booms into it. 'Genesis tells us that when Jehovah made men during the seven days of creation, he made us superior to animals. Therefore, in our behaviour we should not act like animals. Therefore, we must not imitate their mating habits. The principle is clear. We must have sex face to face and not from behind.'

Tracey side-eyes me. I bite down hard on the side of my tongue. Water comes to my eyes. I must not laugh, even a half-titter would be heard. Mom would reach over and slap me on the leg. Worse still, afterwards I would be cornered by a Ministerial Servant or an older, married Sister and counselled, cautioned and possibly, if there is an absence of repentance, reprimanded. And anyway, we are not at the end.

'Question 19, Question C, homosexuality. What did Paul have to say? Yes, Brother Warwick?'

Again, Brother Warwick's passions are stirred and he raises a flapping hand to joyously proclaim homosexuality to be an abomination, evil, debased, contrary to God's Law, to natural law, and it opens the floodgates. Everyone joins in. Hands fly up quoting Paul's energetic writings on human hierarchy – children, women, men who lie with men – and we're sliding easily now, on the home straight, all the way to the necessity of keeping the congregation clean, when Francis Thornton puts up his hand.

There is something lovely about Francis Thornton. He's middle-aged and dusty and English and slightly hunched. He's quite-but-not-very posh and he smells of books and cupboards, rugs and faded watercolours. He comes to the meetings with a stained leather briefcase and a mother and a sister who wear tweeds and cardigans and head-scarves against the wind. They sit next to each other about five rows from the front, modest in all things, a sort of quiet goodness emanating from them wherever they are.

They talk to everyone, black, white, in between, rich, poor, in between. They are monstrously clever but they wear it lightly, often walking part of the way home with us because they live in Moseley as well but not on our side. They used to have the Tuesday meeting at their house, a cottage with leaded windows and black beams in the ceiling. It smelt of cake and wax polish, it smelt of old-fashioned pink flowers and book dust. It smelt of England. We stayed behind one summer night when everyone else had gone and Francis's mother, Agatha, gave Mom a glass of sherry and a tiny biscuit. She doesn't look down on my mother and she always asks after Dad, even though she's never met him and knows he doesn't believe in Jehovah.

When you talk, the Thorntons listen and take you seriously; sometimes they make an English joke, restrained and so dry you only get it the next day.

Sylvia, the sister, is older than Francis and looks more or less like her mother. She has grey hair in a neat bun and always wears a bright-blue cloisonné brooch that I badly want to touch.

Francis has been a Jehovah's Witness since he was twenty, when his father died. The day after the funeral a nice lad knocked the door and said that God had a plan to resurrect the dead not to heaven but back to earth, a paradise earth, made clean and good by the removal of Satan and all those who follow him.

Francis told his bereaved mother and sister and they were all baptized within the year.

So when he puts his hand up at the meeting, he reminds us of God's love for his creation, that it is the act that is not allowed, that people have feelings and all feelings come from God and all people are different. But there are follow-up answers from the extra-zealous who pepper their comments with 'the wrath of God' and 'everlasting death with no resurrection'. Feelings can be mastered with prayer and if your eye offends you, or any other part of your body, cut it off.

We end with the exhortation that anyone 'struggling' can seek the help of an elder, that prayer is free, but meanwhile keep yourself buttoned up and cross-legged.

But Francis has an engineer's mind that is hard to turn off and homosexuality is only one of the questions that he has bottled up, tamped down and shoved aside. They start to rise to the surface. He begins, in his lovely, intelligent way, to gently wonder. One Sunday afternoon, we are behind him leaving the Kingdom Hall when he stops at the door and holds a finger up.

'Polar bears?' he says to himself. 'I wonder. Presumably Noah went overland from the Middle East and collected two of those for the Ark. And Australia for koala bears. Possibly in a boat. Hmm. Rattlesnakes. The Chinese crocodile lizard. Would have been quite a number of journeys for Noah and his sons. Years. Hundreds of them.'

I'm far too desperate to get out of the building to pay much attention. Everyone knows that Jehovah would have made sure that Noah had two of everything, birds, insects, lions, the lot. How He made sure is a matter of faith. And anyway, it's Sunday afternoon and home time.

Over the months that follow, Francis becomes more untidy and distracted. He seems to age and hunch over, wears a hunted look like there's an invisible enemy nearby and, at the end of the meetings, Sylvia always holds him by his elbow and leads him away. Everyone thinks he has cancer.

'Nipples,' he says one summer evening on our walk home. 'Makes you wonder, doesn't it, why Jehovah put nipples on men?'

Tracey nudges me and tries not to laugh.

'I mean,' he continues, 'we believe in creation, that Jehovah had a plan, that He never intended men to breastfeed. That was what woman was created for. So why, I wonder, did He put nipples on Adam?'

No one says anything. His mother and sister have their heads down. We walk on in silence.

'It couldn't be evolution, could it?'

One Thursday evening, the usual programme of talks is abandoned. Brother Davidson climbs the stage.

'We are having a special talk this evening. A talk about apostasy.'

Nothing – not Armageddon, not the eternal and everlasting death of every non-Witness, not adultery, fornication or theft – can compete for sheer horror with the idea of apostasy.

A terrible, ice-cold hush creeps through row after row in the Kingdom Hall until the room is completely silent. Even the babies know not to cry.

Brother Davidson's voice has dropped a few notes.

'Apostasy is a sin against the Holy Spirit for which there is no forgiveness,' he starts. 'There is no resurrection. There is no light. And there are apostates among us.'

Not a sound. Not a murmur.

'There are people who publish books and tracts, write articles in magazines and newspapers that speak against God's Kingdom and the means by which He keeps His people informed. Speaking against the Watchtower Bible and Tract Society is apostasy. And all those who question the dispensation of its light are apostates.'

I quickly do a rough scan of all my misdemeanours.

'Jehovah's Faithful and Discreet Slave in Brooklyn Bethel read all this material. They read articles that speak against God's teachings and against the *Watchtower* and

Awake magazines. They read these things so you don't have to. What would be the benefit for any of Jehovah's Witnesses to read books that God's servants are certain would rock and undermine your faith? Nothing. No bene- fit. See how God loves us? See how He makes sure we are kept safe from harmful thoughts?'

At the end of the meeting, another elder takes the stage. He announces that Francis Thornton is disfellowshipped. He will not be spoken to. He will not be looked at. He will not be acknowledged. He is cast from the light. His mus- ings on nipples have found him out.

The Thorntons are there as usual, warned in advance yet turning up to bow their heads and sag under the con- gregation's collective disapproval. The last song is sung in hushed tones, the prayer is brief. We shuffle out into the dark and watch as the Thorntons walk home without us.

Dad comes home while we're talking about the disfel- lowshipping. Over the years he's heard it all, the scriptures, the doctrine, the living forever, the time of the end. He never says anything, good or bad, doesn't want to know. This time, he stands and listens and then turns to my mother.

'You call this paradise?' he says.

'It's for his own good,' she answers, but she can't meet his eye.

Dad kisses his teeth good and long and looks at us. 'Your mother is a crazy woman, she is.'

22

Beans on Toast

There's a wedding at the Kingdom Hall. It's a teen wedding, he's nineteen and she's eighteen, the inevitable consequence of no sex before marriage, courting done in threes and petting confined to the imagination. The reception is at the local community centre, a bring-a-dish affair and the much-longed-for interruption of a celebration-free Jehovah's Witness year. The West Indian women do us proud: there are trays of fried chicken, vats of coleslaw in rainbow colours, rice salad, potato salad, cakes and tarts and trifles. There is tame dancing and a lot of sitting around the dance floor watching children getting tired. There are never, ever any new boys.

Finding a Jehovah's Witness mate is a three-round contest.

Round 1: Eliminate the talent closest to hand, starting in your own congregation. This is a quick knockout round and not difficult because you've grown up with one another and have, by tacit agreement, dismissed them before they've had their first pimple. In our congregation there is a boy who fancies me. He wears a check suit and has acne so bad Dean calls him Beans on Toast.

Round 2: Scout the nearby congregations. Again, not difficult. All you have to do is visit on a Sunday, sit near the back and see what's what. There's a break in the middle of

the meeting and there's always the preaching hour afterwards when there's mingling and ogling. True, everyone
knows why hormonal teenagers really turn up and it's
not to help with the proselytizing. There's always a frisson
of expectation and excitement when fresh young things
appear in the Kingdom Hall.

You have to do your best to look holy and innocent
enough not to be intercepted by the inevitable congregation busybody and full-time custodian of virgins, yet
fashionable and with-it enough to attract the attention of
the opposite sex.

One Sunday, me and Tracey take two buses to Aston
congregation where we hear there are nice boys with big
afros. We walk in and pretend to be looking for seats. A
stout sister in a flowery polyester dress and American tan
tights is on us in a moment.

'Hello,' she says, hand offered. 'Are you Sisters?'

'Yes, we're from Moseley Congregation, Sister.'

'I see. Welcome, Sisters. There's a special talk today on
the lessons we can learn from Noah's faithfulness at the
time of the end.'

'Yes, we've come to hear it,' I say. 'Isn't Brother Random
giving the talk? We heard his address on "Lot's Wife and
the True Cost of Doubt" at the Assembly.'

'I see, Sister.'

She looks us up and down for signs of appropriate mod-
esty, spirituality, a proper Ministry Bag, sensible shoes,
discreet make-up and any hint of taking the piss.

Tracey is quick. 'And, of course, we'll be on the ministry
afterwards, Sister.'

'Excellent, Sisters. It's good to see young ones who hunger and thirst for righteousness.'

'Yes, we're hungry and thirsty, all right,' says Tracey under her breath.

The best place to sit for our purposes is near enough to the front to be seen by the talent and to look serious about your faith but not too close so you look like some zealous pioneer and killjoy. But you can't be too close to the back, either. That way you look shallow and flighty and give the game away.

Inevitably, there's no one there, no handsome black boys with afros, no lean-limbed white boys with floppy hair, nothing to make the heart beat faster, just some bad suits and side partings who actually do want to talk about King David's perfectly innocent man-love for Jonathan and how many hours they spent knocking doors in the tower blocks of the inner city. And all the rest of them are newly recruited zealots hungry for redemption or too young or too old or too spoken for.

Round 3: The four-day annual summer convention, thousands strong, a whoopee bonanza of new truths, magazines, books, pamphlets hot off the press and young ones a-go-go.

It's always held in a football or rugby stadium in the middle of the summer, prime scouting territory. All you need is a different outfit for each day, some sturdy yet somehow non-Witness walking shoes and a fixed grin. Every single young person over fourteen or under forty-one spends the lunch hour roaming the stadium, eyes scanning and locking, scanning and locking, chatting and evaluating meaningless words designed to fathom the depth of your commitment to the truth versus the possibilities of forbidden good times. There's text and sub-text. By the time you're sixteen you can recognize each other at thirty paces and you're fluent in doublespeak.

It's Twickenham Rugby Stadium, South Stand, near the burger bar. I spot Dave Lewis. Dave Lewis spots me.

'Hi, Mandy. Long time no see.' (I've been round this stadium three times and only just spotted you. Looking good, Sister!)

'Yeah, hi, Brother Lewis, isn't it? Good to see you. What a great talk this morning on washing our sins in the blood of the Lamb.' (Still ugly, Dave, mate. Let me establish my credentials as a no-nonsense, card-carrying good girl with her mind on the ministry. Nothing doin' here.)

'Yeah, call me Dave. What do you think about the new publication they've just announced, "Reaching Out in the Time of the End"?' (Want to phone a friend?)

'Oh, I'm so excited about it. In fact, I got a sneak preview from someone who had been to the first assembly of the season and got an early copy. It's wonderful, especially the chapter on guarding ourselves with the breastplate of righteousness, based on Ephesians, chapter 6, verses 5 to 11.' (Queen to Bishop 5.)

'Wonderful. Look forward to seeing you next year, Sister.' (Just spotted Annette 36C Johnson, got to dash.)

'Jehovah willing! Take care now!' (Next year? Neither of us will last that long, Dave, but whatever.)

23

What's Your Next Move?

The only good food that ever appears in the house comes from my father's hands. Sometimes Mom is at work, sometimes she's ironing or tidying up, and Dad shuffles into the kitchen and starts. He never uses a recipe or consults a book. He sends one of us down Stratford Road for supplies or comes home from work with what he needs. He moves between the sink and the stove, talking to himself while he chops and stirs. He makes what he's been brought up on: neck of lamb, curry, soup with dumplings, Johnny Cakes fried in lard, broiled pork steaks with oily rice, a strange, sweet coconut pudding wrapped in banana leaves called *kanki*, cornmeal with okra.

'Yes, a nice stewed chicken,' he says. 'Skin the bird, put in some garlic and thyme. Not too much salt.'

If he's in a good mood, he tells us about St Kitts and his life there while he cooks, before we get a chance to slink away.

'We was poor. We had to fish every day but not every day you catch something.'

He's scraping the scales off a pink-skinned fish, the pearly circles flying off on to his hand. 'You don't get anything here like we have at home. You need the sun and you don't get sun in England.'

He half tries to make us interested, giving us little jobs under his exacting eye. 'Put them tight in the dish, like so, with pepper. Good.'

We mock his sing-song West Indian accent behind his back. 'Pass me de tometto sauce, no?' we chime just out of his hearing or 'I just want little, little rice with dis' or 'Mus come mek me a samwitch.' Dean has it down to a T, all his mannerisms and inflections.

He makes souse, pig's trotters with fresh lemons and limes, smashed garlic with thyme, finely sliced onions and a fresh chilli in half of the stock. It takes hours, the smell of boiling pigskin permeating every fibre of the house. We wander the kitchen and take the lid off the pot, wait for the skin to come away from the bone revealing shards of pink meat and fat begging to be picked at. In more delicate households, the flesh would be stripped from the trotter and served cold with cucumber and anonymity. Not in ours. The whole thing, or as much as I can get, is dumped in my bowl and I hold the trotter in my hands, pick the pink flesh from the fat and suck the marrow from the bones.

But this is only at the weekends and only the weekends when he's not working. All the rest of the time we have to rely on our mother to feed us. She gives us bread and beans and spaghetti hoops and instant mash and Spam and Weetabix if there's milk to spare and toast if there's bread, and in the absence of meals we roam the house for ingredients and eat them instead. Oxo cubes that remind us of meat, vinegar on stale bread that reminds us of chips, sugar by the spoonful, evaporated milk.

She cooks one meal a day and it's for him. She boils rice to a sludge and curries lamb with not enough spice, ladling it, grey and stringy, on to an enormous plate. She pours on half a tin of carrots and peas and then covers the dish with a Pyrex lid and puts it on a pan of simmering water to wait for him. The smell fills the house. We come down one by one to lift the lid and dip in a finger, taste the juice. But there's only enough dinner for one and we can't risk a chunk of meat or a spoonful of rice because he'd miss it and we'd be in trouble.

Dad's on a late shift so she sends me and Tracey down to the terminus to deliver his dinner. She packs it in a wide-mouthed flask and screws the lid on tight. She wraps it in a tea towel and stuffs it in a duffle bag.

'Walford Road. Wait for him. And don't speak to anyone. A couple of teenage girls are a magnet to some men.'

It's dark outside. We get the bus and walk to the terminus of the number 8 and lean against the wall of a pub. The first bus that comes is driven by Smiler, so black you can hardly see him in the cab.

'Your father is two buses behind me,' he calls through the window. 'Ten minutes, girls.'

The next bus is driven by What's-Your-Next-Move, my dad's friend and chatterbox. He gets out and lights a cigarette, looks us up and down, points the tip of the fag at us and starts.

'You girls coming down with your father's dinner is a good thing. You looking after him. Girls like you need to show respect to your father. Girls like you need to have a plan. You bring food, you go home, you go to school, you grow up. You got to have a plan. Time can run away with you without a plan. One time I did see . . .'

He goes on without a break so there is no need to have an answer until right at the end. We wait politely while he delivers his homily, one we have heard many times.

He takes the last drag and screws the butt under his black boots.

'People that prosper are the ones that are prepared for life! You don't go to bed to dream. You go to bed to plan! That's what you must do. So when someone ask you what's your next move, you always have an answer.'

'Yes, Jim,' we say. 'Thank you.'

'Good. You father soon come.'

He waves and we wave back. When Dad's bus comes, and all the people get off, we hand over the duffle bag. He looks inside. 'Good,' he says. He digs in his pocket and gives us some change.

'Thanks, Dad.'

'Straight home,' he says.

But we're in no hurry. We walk the long way back down Stoney Lane and Ladypool Road looking like two girls about town, like we might live in a flat somewhere and not have to go home at all. We spend our bus fare and the money from Dad on ten Park Drive, the cheapest cigarettes in the shop. We light one each and practise holding it between our fingers. Now up in the air. Now swinging by our side. We look great. We look older. The fag tastes like damp wood, harsh and bitter, and I blow it out as quick as I can. Tracey's better than me and has been practising at school. She blows smoke rings as we walk and manages to keep her cigarette alight until there's only an inch left. We play 'When We're Sixteen' and we know our lines.

'When we're sixteen we can leave home,' she says. We're only fifteen months apart.

'We can get a flat in Moseley Village,' I say. 'We can have parties and buy a three-piece suite.'

'We won't have to go to the meetings.'

'We can go to the pub. We can have boyfriends.'

We both know what that means. We remember Francis Thornton, who no one speaks to or speaks about, who we heard had some kind of breakdown and has never been back to the meetings. He has never found the fortitude to turn up at the Kingdom Hall for months and months with no one speaking to him so that the elders can see how repentant he is. He has never sung the last song then walked out while no one catches his eye and done this a hundred times, two hundred, until the elders decide he's sorry enough and has learned the error of his ways and had a good long taste of humiliation and disgrace.

'If we get disfellowshipped,' Tracey says after a pause, 'Mom won't be able to speak to us.'

'I think she still would, though, don't you?'

'No,' says Tracey. 'Not to me, anyway.'

We link arms and trudge up Ladypool Road, the ghost of Black Nana between us. Her arms open for Tracey and my mother saying no. Black Nana leaving without her and my mother's triumph.

We saunter up Church Road with another cigarette apiece, slightly sick of them now, perfecting our plans, fermenting our freedom until it bubbles up on the horizon almost within touching distance. We cut across the side roads of Moseley Village to take the long way down the hill of Woodlands Road towards home.

The cigarettes will last us for weeks, one each, every time we can get away from home to sit in the far corner of the park on a damp and splintered bench watching cars drive through the ford, hoping they get stuck in the middle, talking all the time about a future of fags, discos and boyfriends.

The next day, they're arguing. Dad's diabetes is out of control. It took months for them to diagnose his losing weight, his tiredness, but no one is surprised it's diabetes, the thing that killed Black Nana when she went home. My mother is full of late wisdom.

'You've got it from eating chocolate bars while you're driving, Arthur. You've got it from eating too much on an empty stomach.'

Dad is quietly and persistently disobedient and Mom loudly and persistently reminds him of the rules.

'I keep telling you, Arthur. You can't have Hermesetas in custard with a sponge pudding, that's not what they're for.'

'They said no sugar. I ain't having sugar.' He sits back on the kitchen chair, an empty bowl in front of him, his hands over his belly.

'What do you think the sponge pudding is made of? You'll kill yourself the way you're going.'

'Then you all can bring me back, ain't it? The resurrection or whatever you call it.' He winks at me. 'I rise from the dead straight into paradise, isn't it, Sheilo? Diabetes done.'

'Don't make fun of it, Arthur. It's going to happen. It's in the Bible.'

'Oh, oh! In the Bible.'

She stops washing up and faces him. 'What about your paradise? You saving up every penny you earn and building that bloody house in St Kitts while this one falls down around our ears? I suppose that's all right, is it? Your kids in jumble-sale clothes while you stock up on suit lengths so you can strut around the West Indies.'

His face wears a terrible look. The house in St Kitts is his dream, his reason for being, his reason to work, his reason to go home, his reason for coming here in the first place and the reason he doesn't feed us and dress us, the reason Mom goes to work and tries to run the house on coppers, the reason he has to look good and be different and not go out and waste money on drink. The reason he breathes.

He sits between me and the stairs, and I dare not move and get caught in the crossfire. She continues.

'I'm working my fingers to the bone and doing everything with my money while you're keeping yours to yourself,' she says.

Dad speaks quietly. 'When I come here, it was only to go back. I tell you that long time.'

'You've had kids since then, Arthur.'

'They can come.'

'And what about me? I suppose I'm not invited?'

'You can come if you want. I'm going home, Sheila. I tired tell you. I'm going home.'

'You make me sick,' she says under her breath, but we all hear.

Dad stands up. He towers over her, six foot six versus five foot two. 'My paradise will come before yours, Sheila.'

She starts to cry.

'If only I had a one-bedroomed flat,' she sniffs. 'I just want to live on my own. I've had enough.'

She shoves past us. She puts her coat on. She gets her Ministry Bag. And then the door slams. She will be out for hours. She will knock the doors of neighbours and strangers and tell them about the good news of the Kingdom, clutching her Bible and turning the pages with shaking hands.

24

Half a Box of Chocolates

Mom's got a new friend. Whenever Mom gets a new friend, it's all we hear about.

'Linda's coming today, run and get some custard creams.'

'Linda's little dog went to the vet for an injection.'

'Linda's having her hedge trimmed.'

Linda comes round with gossip and half a box of chocolates and they sit in the kitchen with everlasting coffees and hushed voices. They chat and laugh, and afterwards Mom's in a good mood for ages, editing and repeating the highlights.

'Linda's got a new job at the fruit-and-veg shop. She said the manager's very handsy. And you know how attractive she is.'

Each friend lasts a season of about three years before there's a falling-out or an argument or Mom's cloying love makes them run away. There's been Sue and Salma, Linda, Marg, Madge, and now Mom's new friend is June. There's a goodbye party for someone at work and Mom's getting ready to go to it with June.

She opens the door to the telly room to say goodbye. She's made a terrible effort and even we can see she's overdone it. There's some kind of hairpiece at the back, inches of eyeliner and false eyelashes that make her look like a man in drag. Karen is only nine and sees with a child's eye.

'Oh, Mom, you look beautiful!' she says.

Mom sniffs and turns around. 'What do you think, Arthur?'

Dad looks up from the telly and squints in her direction. He can't help it.

'Take care nobody take you for one of them, whatcha-callit, endangered animal there, Sheilo.'

'What?'

'We was just watching it on the news, there, wasn't we?' he says to all of us in complete innocence. 'You didn't hear about it? They is looking for a panda to mate with that one they got there in China? Look, your eyes, Sheilo! Look your eyes? You better watch out. Kim! Kim! Remind me if you mother not back by midnight, we go look for her at Dudley Zoo come morning.'

She laughs with the red gash of her mouth but it's thin and false.

As soon as she goes out, Dad might send Dean to the shop for some sweets or chocolate and he'll share it out, keeping most of it for his diabetic self.

It's Tarzan on the telly. There are many Tarzans. There's Herman Brix, Lex Barker and Ron Ely, but this week it's Johnny Weissmuller, the American Olympic swimmer whose loincloth is cut to show off his magnificent legs. He's swinging from rope to rope across the African jungle, high up above the wild animals circling the jungle floor below. If he falls, they will eat him.

Sooner or later, we get to the scene in every Tarzan film where he's meeting the native chief with the always-wicked witch doctor who tries to put in a bad word for the white man. The witch doctor's face is only partially visible because he's wearing the entire skin of a bear, head, paws and all, and he has a bone through his nose. He also has the obligatory spear that he keeps banging on the dusty floor outside the chief's hut.

The chief, who is a kindly, blacked-up American actor we've seen in lots of other films as a cowboy or Mexican, wants Tarzan to help them because without him and his special monkey calls they risk the wrath of bad white hunters who don't respect black people the way the American does. The chief talks to Tarzan in his own language. Tarzan answers in broken English but the chief manages to understand.

Tarzan is friends with all the natives and all the monkeys, but his favourite is Cheetah, the chimpanzee who holds Tarzan's hand while he, as King of the Jungle, organizes international relations among the savages. At the inevitable climax of the film Tarzan will have to do some wild swimming so Johnny Weissmuller can show off his Olympic freestyle and diving skills, then as soon as he emerges from the crocodile-infested river he will do the African version of yodelling and call the elephants to pull some trees down to stop the money-grabbing Westerners from doing something bad.

We're bored with the story we have seen a hundred times. Dean nudges me but speaks to Dad.

'Is it really like that, Dad?'

'What?'

'In the jungle? I mean, is it dangerous?'

Dad sips his punch and says nothing. His silence means

we can carry on. I'm up next. 'Did you live in one of those huts, Dad? Didn't you get wet when it rained?' I say.

'What you all talking about?' he says but keeps his face to the screen.

Then Tracey's turn. 'How many lions did you kill, Dad?'

He turns his head slowly and we all go quiet. He stares at his English children and kisses his teeth. He stands and faces us.

'You see me? The leopard them couldn't catch me. And snakes? I just grab up the snake like so and strangle it with my two hands. And crocodiles and bears. Everything. I just throw the spear clean through its heart. That was me.'

We're laughing at his antics as he shows us how to twist a cobra into a knot and dash it to the jungle floor. *Bam!* He grabs up the panther and breaks its jaw before it can eat him. *Bam!*

'Yes!' he says. 'It just like that in the West Indies. Zebra and giraffe, every damn thing. We don't have houses.' His voice has changed. 'No! It look just like that there with the straw roof. Yes! You didn't know? The witch doctor doing ju-ju dance all day. And the women them with they breast out, just like that. Yes. Fighting tigers all day is what we do.'

He isn't joking. His voice is cold and hard. No one laughs. We turn back to the television when he sits down in his chair. We watch the end of the film in silence.

25

That's What It's Like to be a Woman

Now, there are days on end when Mom's in a bad mood. She goes to work as an auxiliary nurse at Dudley Road Hospital, volunteering for every unpopular shift, every weekend night shift, Friday, Saturday, Sunday, eight at night until eight in the morning. She earns extra money and gets away from the house. And all week she complains about Dad to anyone who will listen, complains about her life.

She goes to work. She tidies up. She goes out on the ministry. She comes home. She makes Dad's dinner. And in between she tell us all the things she has to put up with from him, his meanness and penny-pinching, his lack of affection, his idleness.

'We had the chance to buy the house next door,' she says while she cleans the windows. 'I said to him, "Arthur," I said, "just think of it. Live in one and rent the other one out." But not him. Oh no. Couldn't bear to see his bank balance go down even if it is for a good cause. And anyway, what do I know? I'm only a thick Irish paddy. Not like the big Arthur O'Loughlin. I used to bring home my wage packet and give it to him unopened. Unopened! Bloody idiot.'

She shakes her head and looks off into the distance. You can't leave the room, you can't agree, you can't disagree. You have to keep quiet and keep listening.

'I mean, what kind of fool helps her husband buy a house in another country? What idiot would help him make a life for himself somewhere else? Me, that's who.'

She notices me and points a finger.

'You make sure you don't make the same mistake I did. Marry a man who gets up off his backside once in a bloody while and helps around the house. Marry a man who can make you happy, who's got more to him than cricket and the bloody telly.'

She starts crying or disappears somewhere in the house or down the road, and when she comes home, she makes us tidy up or put the washing on or wash the dishes or read the *Watchtower* or turn the bloody telly off or play with the kids or sweep the path or clean the windows or go outside. Just go outside.

Her disappearing becomes more regular. She starts brushing her hair and finding excuses to go to the shop. She grabs her purse and bag and says, 'Back in five minutes,' but it's more like half an hour. She starts dropping a name into conversation, Ned, a neighbour down Passey Road, a nice man with a lovely front garden, a black man. It takes ages for us to cotton on.

One day, she sends me and Karen to the shop for some bread. 'Go down to MacFisheries,' she says, which is unusual because it's not the cheapest and it's out of the way but I don't mind because I've nicked some money and I'll be able to buy a Marathon bar and eat it in peace, taking my time.

On our way down Passey Road, I see him, this tall man with a trilby, with a trowel and a white shirt open at the collar. He says hello when we pass and seems to recognize Karen. She waves at him.

We get the bread and, on our way home, we pass him again. He's leaning on the gate this time.

'Sweet?' he says, rattling something in a paper bag.

We take one each and as we stand there he tells us what he's planting: flowers for shade, flowers for colour, red and orange to remind him of home.

'Guyana,' he says. 'Beautiful country. How is your mother?'

I see my father in him, the yearning for home and the slow working of the jaw, but he's softer and rounder, scruffier as well. He's nice and seems really interested in us.

'She's fine, thank you.'

He goes as if to speak, to say something, but changes his mind.

'Say hello from me,' he says.

There's a sort of question in my mind about him but I can't reach it. Karen rushes home and tells Mom she saw Uncle Ned. Mom flushes red and looks at me with frightened eyes.

'It's OK,' I say, 'we only took one sweet each.' I think she's worried that we've disgraced her with our greed or bad manners but she grabs her purse and is out of the door in a flash.

'I forgot to tell you to get some sugar.'

She's gone for ages and when she comes home she's out of breath like she's walked for miles. She slumps into a kitchen chair and throws her purse on the table. No sugar in her hand.

'What is it he says?' she asks me.

'Who?'

'Your father.'

'I don't know.'

'Yes, you do. "Your mother is a crazy woman." That's what he thinks of me and he's right. What did I expect? I thought I had a way out. I thought . . . What did I think? All men are the same, aren't they? They're all promises and sunshine, but you still get wet, don't you? It's all bloody drizzle at the end of the day. I'm stupid, that's what I am.'

She makes a cup of coffee and sits staring out of the window, tears in her eyes, her pale face red and lined.

Every so often, Mom will collect milk bottles. Three pints get delivered every day. She washes two bottles and puts them out the front for the milkman. The last one is placed outside the back door in a neat and tidy row. It goes on for weeks. Eventually she starts stacking them in an old plastic laundry basket. We watch it fill up with the empties. It's only a matter of time.

It will be a Saturday morning when the house is a mess, when there's no food in the cupboards, when she's been looking after other people's children all week and still got nothing to show for it, when Karen needs new shoes and Kim needs a new coat, when the electricity bill comes in and the catalogue money won't cover it, when two of us have been arguing and another one complains about the cold.

She waits until Dad's gone to work then opens the back

door and hauls the clanking laundry basket outside into the concrete yard.

She looks calm. She selects a milk bottle from the pile, picks it up and throws it with all her might against the wall of the outhouse and watches it smash into tiny pieces. She bites her tongue between her teeth and picks up another one and throws it again. We stare out of the upstairs window. You can smell the fight, hear her grunt and grunt and exhale as she works her way through the bottles, one after another, sweating, staring, single-minded. It makes a kind of music, the bottles and the sound of her fury. When the basket is empty, she goes inside and fetches the broom. She's fine then for a few days.

Sometimes I'm watching the street from the front-room window and I see her coming up the road in her nurse's uniform. She has her head slightly to the side, like she's listening to some silent music. She walks with small steps, slowly, precisely, carefully, because she's done a twelve-hour shift on the maternity ward at Dudley Road Hospital. She'll have stopped at the market on the way home, bought a pint of milk to make sure she gets the cream for her coffee. Maybe bought a custard tart. Even though she's dog-tired, there's still no rush to come home.

I see her. I see her beige woolly hat pulled down low, her dark-brown coat with a high-buttoned neck and her dark-brown lace-ups with the spongy soles, the better for creeping round sleeping women and brand-new babies. I see her square hands, cold and mottled, gripping her sensible bag full of market bargains and bruised fruit, and I see her brokenness and her stories, like they are written on her face, bowing her down, overlooked by her mother, unloved by my father, and the combined five of us not enough to plug the hole those two have made.

She's cold and white-faced as she puts the key in the door.

'Hello, Mom,' I say.

'I'm freezing,' she says as she walks down the hall into the kitchen. I follow. Sometimes she sits for ages in her coat and hat with a mug in her hands while me, Tracey and Kim tidy up around her.

'Them black nurses,' she says with her thin lips, 'they're so lazy. They don't do anything till the last minute. They leave me and June to do all the worst jobs.'

We – the black women she has made – look at her, but she just carries on.

'They don't really talk to me and June. They don't like white women who marry black men. They talk to each other and leave us out. You know what they're like. Jamaicans, most of them. The Africans aren't so bad.'

Sometimes it's Asians. 'Talk in their own language. Some of them are just girls, teenagers on their third or fourth baby. And the husbands are all middle-aged men. That's how they do it in their country so they think it's all right to bring it over here.'

Sometimes it's stuck-up English women, white managers, anyone with a foreign accent, men who don't turn up for the birth, men who do and get in the way, women on their seventh, women who smoke.

Other times she tells us about the babies born with terrible faces, with no arms, three arms. She tells us, her virgin daughters, about the screaming hours of child-birth, forceps, vaginal rips and anal stitches. She tells us about wide-eyed men and babies born silent, the never-screaming ones in the private rooms, families outside in the corridor, all of them weeping. And young women going home alone, their big empty bellies, their leaking breasts and the bagfuls of tiny white outfits they leave behind.

'I saw something terrible last night,' she says in a hushed voice. 'When the mother saw it, she burst into tears. Couldn't tell you if it was a boy or a girl but we have to ask them if they want to see.'

We are torn between listening and running away, between life and death and Mom as witness.

'You don't want them to see but they don't believe you. And then that's their baby, that's what they'll remember. They don't live long, them babies, and it's a blessing. Dads are worse than the mothers sometimes. They just walk away or cry and they have to be comforted by the woman. Think about that. Think about comforting a grown man when your baby's dead. That's what it's like to be a woman. You have to think of everyone before yourself.'

Eventually, she goes to bed, pulling the curtains together and closing the door. 'Don't let me sleep past three,' she says as she walks upstairs. 'I've got to go out on the ministry and get my hours in.'

The house must be quiet while she sleeps, the telly on low, no arguments or banging doors. She wakes and comes downstairs, paler than she was before. She's dressed for knocking doors, almost the same clothes but neater some-how, browner, beiger and more Christian.

She has her special Ministry Bag with a thousand pockets for leaftlets, pens and 'Not at Home' slips, for this magazine and that magazine and a special place for her Bible. She needs to be able to whip it out at a moment's notice.

She opens the front door with a sigh.

'I'm meeting June at the top of the road. We're doing "Not at Homes" for a couple of hours.'

I stand at the window and watch her walk away, careful steps, careful shoes, a leaflet in her hand that she hopes to give to a passer-by so she can start the clock as quickly as possible and offer the sacrifice of two cold February hours to the exacting Jehovah.

We breathe easier with her gone.

26

I'm Pregnant

My mother was the second of nine children and had to help with looking after the others, doing jobs around the house to keep it from falling apart. Nan took in lodgers, Irishmen from the building sites and factories, who got two meals a day and a bed in a shared bedroom in a cavernous two-storey flat above an old shop that spanned a whole corner of Stratford Road. Nine children, two parents and as many working men as you could squeeze in the gaps. There was always cooking and cleaning and bed-changing to be done and those were the children's jobs, boys as well as girls, though it was only the girls who had to be kept safe from the homesick, sex-starved young men from the fields of Munster.

I'm pegging out the washing with my mother one day and she starts telling me about Nan's savage eye.

'Oh, she would watch you and make sure you were decent or in bed before they came back from the pub. She'd shoo you out of the way if the lodgers were around and if you were helping in the kitchen she had her eyes on everyone. Not that we knew why. You couldn't know about the birds and the bees in those days,' she tells me. 'It was practically a sin to know about sex, you'd be condemned.'

She passes me one end of a candy-striped sheet. It's so worn in the middle that it's almost transparent and won't last another round with the twin tub.

'We had this one lodger,' she continues, staring off into the distance, leaving me to tangle with the sheet on my own, trying to keep it from dragging on the dusty garden path. 'Oh, he was a looker. You get these Irish sometimes with black hair and blue eyes, something to do with the Spanish Armada . . .'

Nothing then while she clomps down memory lane, up the backstairs to the flat above 516 Stratford Road, through the heavy wooden doors and into the steaming kitchen.

'Logan something,' she says. 'Or something Logan. Your grandmother used to have all the men sit on a bench for breakfast, all squashed up together so she could get more round the table. She'd put the rashers and bread down and they'd need to be quick. Tea and sugar and milk. Half past seven in the morning and we girls would have to be up, helping and clearing away. We'd walk in between them, putting down plates and collecting them and never saying a word unless it was to Mom. She had her eyes on us, one baby on her hip, Kevin round her feet and all the rest of us to look after on her own. Your grandfather would be sitting at the table himself.'

She smiles. 'One day, Logan is sitting on the end of the bench and he looks up and catches my eye and smiles. No one else sees. And that was me in love. Ah, he's just a boy when you think about it, probably eighteen or something, and if he was going to have the eye for anyone it would have been my sister Mary with the looks, not me with my broken nose.'

She sniffs. There's a detour she could take here, an easy slip down the bitter lanes of her childhood where she's the runt of the litter, not as pretty as one sister, not as clever as another, where Mary has all the boys wanting her and Mom has only her piety and good nature to recommend her which, when you are sixteen, counts for less than nothing – in truth, counts against you. But, for a change, she resists and puts her foot back on the story.

'Anyway, we had to clear up, me and Greta. She must have been sixteen at the time, so I'm fifteenish. Anyway, he was always last out of the door, Logan was. All of the men would tramp down the stairs to wait outside The Bear where they'd get picked up by the vans taking them to the building sites. So, there's Logan stuffing some bread down and gulping at his tea. There's no one else around. Mom's gone and Greta's gone, and it's just me and him, and he stands up. "Grand," he says and winks as he leaves the room. At me. He winks at me. I must have gone red, I don't remember. Anyway, quick as a flash I sat down on his bit of the bench and I felt the warmth of Logan's backside seep right through my dressing gown, right through my night-dress, and into mine. I felt him on my body as though he was still there, like I was sitting on his lap, and I sat and sat until my mother came into the room and told me to get up and wash the dishes.'

She starts laughing then and dips into the washing basket, picking up three things at a time and pegging them on the line like a machine, a fistful of pegs and an armful of knickers.

'Well, I was sobbing by the time I got to our bedroom. Greta was there getting ready for school and I told her. "I'm pregnant," I said. She shook my shoulders and hissed into my face. "Who was it? How do you know? Which one was it?" I was beside myself. "Logan," I said. She threw me down on the bed we shared. "Logan! What a dirty pig! When? How do you know? Where did you do it? Who have you told?" But I'm crying into my hands. Then she sits down and puts her arms around me. "What happened?" she said. "I sat on the bench." "Go on," she said. "And it was warm." "Yes?" "And I could feel him on my arse." Greta took my hands from my face and looked hard at me. "What did he do then?" "He went to work." Silence from Greta and a slow nod of her head. "You sat on his seat? That's it?" she asks. "Yes," I answered. "And I felt the warmth off him." I was beside myself now. Weeping for Ireland. It was beginning to sink in. The shame and the unwanted baby and, worst of all, my mother and the beating I would get. "I stayed there till it went cold," I added, to make sure she knew it was serious. Well, Greta got up and threw my clothes at me. "Get dressed, you bloody idiot. And stop crying. You're not pregnant."'

The washing sags on the long, long plastic washing line that runs the length of the garden path. We take one wooden prop each and, on her count, raise the line high until our skirts and jumpers, shirts and socks, the tea towels and nappies are all dancing in the wind, the sleeves of Dad's shirts filling and making him beckon us to him as he would never do in real life.

'It took me a while to believe her,' Mom continues as we gather the baskets and walk back inside, 'but Greta wouldn't lie. And anyway, as the months came and went I didn't get any fatter and I still got my periods. They were God's guarantee of goodness. That's what we thought. God gave us periods to guard the virgins against violation. Not quite sure how that worked but you never questioned it in those days. The priest was God Himself.'

I marvelled at her ignorance – even I, at fifteen, knew that it took more than a hot seat to get you up the duff.

'Anyhow,' she said as she stuffed the next load of washing into the machine, 'you girls be careful. That's all I'm saying.'

27

I'm Not Living Next Door to Blackies

They are hardly ever together in the same room at the same time. Dad is at work or watching the telly and Mom's at the meeting, on the ministry or tidying up. Dad passes Mom in the hall or the kitchen and says something like 'I going up now' or 'I going out to come back.' She says 'All right' or 'See you later' or sometimes she doesn't answer him at all.

When the other one is out, they tell us stories about their life before us. They both want us as their audience, for the depository of their dreams, for their excuses, justifications, explanations.

Dad's polishing his shoes.

'When my ship land in Portsmouth, we all come off. You know, you had to walk off the ship, a long way to the place where you come out on to the street itself. I come out. I walk. I take it slow, you know. Me never see anything like this place. Everything is strange, you know? I take one look around and I see everybody in black shoes. My shoes is spats. Spats, because it is the fashion back home. A nice pair of spats, my best shoes. But when I see everybody in black shoes, I say, "Oh no, Arthur boy!" I didn't want to stand out and look stupid. So I gone clear to the first shoe shop I see and I ask for a pair of black shoes. So the man look at me and he say, "Oh yes, sir, sit down." So I sit down and then this woman, she come over with a pair of black shoes and she get down to put them on my foot. What a beautiful thing! I never see that before. A white woman get down on her knees to put a pair of shoes on a black man foot.'

Another time, we're in the kitchen waiting for the Johnny Cakes to fry. We ask him about the West Indies and he answers like he's in court making an account of himself.

'Born in Basseterre, St Kitts in the Leeward Islands of the Caribbean, 1928. Arthur Desmond O'Loughlin but they also call me The Rock, Kid Mirror or Lofty but mostly The Rock. I had two brothers, Caesar and Cyril, but Cyril die young. My father was a businessman on the island, he had shops. But my mother was poor and she wasn't married to him. Me and Cyril was his. He didn't give us anything, no money, nothing, so we had to look after ourselves. Me, I get a good idea. I start collecting bottles. You could just go around and find bottles that people throw away and if you collect so many you could take them back to the shop and get money, just a little money, but when you is hungry, a little money can help you survive. Anyway, I used to buy myself a tin of sardines and hide it, and when nobody was around I used to open it and eat it all to myself.'

He stops moving the Johnny Cakes around the pan and puts his head down.

'Cyril died. He got sick and died. He was just a boy. He was hungry as well. I didn't share nothing with Cyril. I didn't think about him.'

He spoons the red, molten corned-beef hash on to five plates and adds a Johnny Cake to each.

'Come,' he says. 'Eat.'

*

Mom is ironing while we're trying to watch a detective programme on the telly. When she's in the mood to reminisce, anything else is pointless. She stands next to the huge laundry basket with a little spray gun that she uses to dampen Dad's cotton shirts. She uses the iron like a punctuation mark.

'You were six weeks old,' she says, smashing the iron into the sleeve, 'and your father decided we'd had enough of living in one room. We could have bought a house in Small Heath easily but not your father. He had better things in mind. You know what he's like. We wanted a nice area away from the Indians and Pakistanis and the Africans. So first of all we went to Acocks Green.'

The sleeve done, she brings out the starch for the collar.

'But every time we turned up and enquired at the estate agent's they said all the houses we wanted to look at had mysteriously been sold or the details weren't available or the people had changed their minds. Then when we did get an appointment to go and look at the house, they took one look at your father and said someone had just bought it or it was off the market. There'd be people looking through curtains, staring at him – and you know what your father's like – proud. Anyway, when we saw this house was for sale he said, "Right, Sheilo, you go on your own. Look at the house, don't tell nobody nothing." So I went and had a look. It was perfect. So I said we'd take it. They didn't know nothing until me and your father turned up. Oh, you should have seen the faces of the neighbours when your father got out of Mike's van! Oh yes! It was too late then! We'd bought it! Clever, your father is. He knew what to expect.'

She puts the white shirt on a wooden hanger and gives it to me to hang over the door. She picks up another one and starts all over again.

'Few months after we moved in, September 1960, three FOR SALE signs go up, both of these next door,' she says, showing us with a point of the iron, 'and them directly opposite. It was too much for them to bear. Here they were, middle of the country, decent working-class people, minding their business, and along comes a short Irish refugee so thick she's living in sin with a six-foot-six enormous black man from Africa who'll murder them all in their beds and at the very least lower the tone of the street.'

She laughs. We laugh with her. Then she's off.

'Imagine them, can't you?' She starts talking in her best Brummie voice.

'*Get on to that estate agent, Maureen, I'm not living next to blackies. What about the kids' school? It will be overrun by Pakis before you know it, speaking their own language, eating their own food. They'll be playing drums morning, noon and night, you watch. It's the children I feel sorry for. They're neither one thing nor the other, half this and half that. Get on to that estate agent, Maureen, and get him up here fast as you can!*'

They turn things up a few notches and try to outdo one another with their holidays. Dad decides to go back to St Kitts for the first time in twenty years. He orders an enormous barrel that he lodges in the front room and starts to fill it with goodies to take home: chocolate, soap, bedclothes, shoes, cups and saucers, pictures, glasses, vases, packets of biscuits and treats we have never seen before.

We creep in from time to time and take something out. There are toys for children he's never met and boxes of toffee and chocolates that he's never brought home to us. There are bedclothes that would fit my bed and glasses that are needed in the kitchen. We are surprised he knows about these things, we are amazed he would spend money on them when all we've ever heard is how broke we are, how we can't afford any of the stuff that would make our house nice or our bellies full.

Still he brings it home, bags of the stuff. In it all goes until the barrel is filled to the brim and someone comes and collects it and sends it off ahead of him. Then he starts having suits made that he brings home and hangs up in suit bags and spends days upon days matching the suit to the shoes and the handkerchief, cufflinks and tiepins. He buys shirts and vests that he tells us to take out of the packet and iron for him. It takes months for him to prepare to go home and not be a disgrace to the adventure.

He gets a six-month open ticket but he's home in two. We barely had time to get used to his absence. Barely had time to relax. He looks tireder and blacker. He's bought us gold-coloured bangles. He's lost some of his luggage or left it behind. It wasn't what he expected, he said. Things had changed in the twenty years he had been away. Nobody to play cards with. Relatives that didn't look after him properly. He's lost weight and confidence, his shoulders sagging under the disappointment.

'It was hot, must have been a heatwave. I don't remember it so hot. You couldn't get good chicken out there. It was just neck and back they had to eat. Everything was too expensive. Nothing on the telly on the island. You couldn't get a good film. Not like when we was young.'

He stops talking about it eventually, after the excuses have run out and he's found a way to make sense of not belonging, of missing *Morecambe and Wise* and *Songs of Praise*, depot gambling nights, damp summer evenings and, unaccountably and unexpectedly, his own children.

As soon as he comes home and they've stopped arguing about it, Mom decides to visit Auntie Mary in Key West. She comes home one day and lays a little cardboard wallet on the kitchen table.

'That's me. There's my tickets. Next Friday week. Eleven hours in the air. That's my holiday.'

She looks at us one by one, defiantly. We say nothing. The envelope stays there all day, untouched, until Dad comes in. He sits next to it and eats his dinner from a big Pyrex dish. Mom's washing up. We wander in and out, waiting for him to say something. He doesn't. He doesn't ask about her plans and she doesn't tell him.

The following week she buys a tartan suitcase and a special padlock and packs half of it with summer clothes we've never seen before, sandals and Irish food for Mary, Ovaltine and Polo mints.

'I'm leaving space in case I want to bring anything back,' she says. 'Do you want anything bringing back,

Arthur? Anything from Florida?' There's a triumph in her voice, a superiority we seldom hear.

He says nothing and the next day Uncle Kevin turns up in his old BMW and drives her all the way to Heathrow Airport.

She spends the whole six weeks in Key West with Auntie Mary and an extra one for good measure. Only Kim bothers with the meetings. Me and Tracey get our first taste of *Top of the Pops* and *Monty Python*. Dean plays air guitar and sings along. He starts forcing his hair into the hairstyles of pop stars. We watch *Steptoe and Son* and *Callan*, Max Bygraves, Mike and Bernie Winters, detective shows and World War Two documentaries until our eyes are gritty and sore. We bask everlastingly in the forbidden thrill of Thursday-night telly and not getting wet on the cold walk to the house meeting on Cotton Lane and the somehow even longer walk back.

Karen sits quietly while we plait her long hair or gossip. She's the one that Mom swears will be different.

'I won't make mistakes with her the way I have with all you lot,' she always says. We are mistakes because we are faithless, because we answer back, but Karen is sweet and does as she's told and was born into The Truth. We're all still wearing it like a stranger's coat, too long, too tight, uncomfortable.

Dad says nothing about us missing the meeting. He knows we don't want to go and, anyway, it means he doesn't have to give us the bus fare and make sure we look decent. Sundays without Mom are lazy days without getting dressed; running down to the paper shop for the *News of the World* for Dad and coming home to an afternoon of war films and gangsters in baggy suits killing each other in black and white.

When Dad's out at work, we have the house to ourselves and no one is in charge, not even Kim. Dad brings home food or tells us to buy bread and sausages. We have scrambled eggs with onion, saltfish and Johnny Cakes. We have cocoa with too much sugar in it and when all the sugar's gone we beg Dad for money to buy more. One of us is always too sick for school and Dad lets us stay home. He doesn't make us tidy up or go to bed on time.

And all the days run into one another until Uncle Kevin brings her back again and she opens her suitcase with a flourish. She's brought home strange-smelling body lotion for her suntan. She's brought afro combs and afro sheen for Kim and Tracey. She's brought leather handbags for the ministry, stuff she found in 'yard sales' and 'thrift stores'. For weeks, she compares her tan with ours and starts saying things like 'Pass me my *purse*,' pointing to her enormous shopping bag, and 'Oh, you can put that paper in the *trash*.'

She tells us about the *yo-ghurt* she ate and how she laddered her *pantyhose*, and if her story hasn't got an Americanism in it, she finds a way to cram one in.

'I just went to the shop and nearly slipped on the *sidewalk*.'

My father winks at us behind her back and when she leaves the room he starts to laugh.

'What me tell you? Your mother is a crazy woman.'

28

Ein Gekochtes Ei

School ends. I'm overjoyed to be on the bus to Garretts Green Technical College. It's about as far away from home as possible without actually ending up in Coventry. Kate said she was going to do secretarial studies so I signed up with her. Two weeks before the start of the course, she told me she wouldn't be going because she'd got taken on as a trainee with the National Westminster Bank. Oh, and she got offered another one with the tax office and another with the Co-operative Funeral Service, but she doesn't want to work with dead people so the bank it is.

I'm pleased for her. I'm disappointed. I'm angry. Kate, behind me in every single subject at school, ninth or tenth when I was first or second. But I can't get a job. Everything I apply for, from basic clerical to shop work in town, is a yes, yes, yes, come for an interview.

So I skip along to the office, clutching my exam certificates, with my hair greased back and my best smile, but as soon as they see me it's the same thing.

'Mandy O'Loughlin?'

'Yes.'

'O'Loughlin?'

'Yes.'

'Isn't that Irish?'

'Yes, my mom's Irish but it's my dad's name.'

'Your dad?'

'Yes.'

'He's . . .'

'West Indian.'

'Right, right. Yes, well . . .'

Every time I slink back home, Dad talks to the black half of me who doesn't get the job: 'You can't trust the white man.'

And I have to sit silent, listening to the same speech that ends up the same way.

'You walk with an umbrella?'

'Yes, Dad.'

'You wear a costume?'

'Yes, Dad.'

'You polish you shoe?

'Yes, Dad.'

He kisses his teeth. 'They give the job to the white girl that come in after you.'

I dreamed I'd be out of the house by now, thought I'd be earning money, that I could get away from Springfield Road, from the two of them with their separate plans for their separate neverlands. So Garretts Green College, seventy minutes from home and seventy minutes back, would have to do.

Lots of the girls know each other but I'm from the other side of town and, without Kate, I'm all alone. I line up outside Room 2H. A black girl is behind me; we do the solidarity smile and she stands closer.

'Couldn't get a job?' she says.

'No. I mean, yes.'

'Me neither. I'm still applying though.'

'And me.'

'I'm Jackie.'

'Mandy,' I say.

A tidy little woman with wavy hair and coral lipstick clicks past us in her kitten heels and unlocks the door. She gestures us inside. Her tartan suit is doll-sized and her face is powdery and pale. But her eyes are black and laser sharp.

'Find a desk, class,' she orders.

The room is set up with desks in rows, every one dominated by a manual typewriter. Right by the door, near the plug socket, there is a single, ultra-modern electric IBM Font Ball typewriter and a tall girl grabs it.

Typewriting. I learn in the first five minutes from Mrs Strick with the slightly Welsh accent that 'typing' is not a word we use. We are in ADVANCED secretarial studies. ADVANCED. We are there because we will be, if we work hard and keep the rules and deport ourselves with grace and discretion, a SECRETARY to a very, very important man, booking his international flights, ordering flowers for his wife, recording very, very important dates in his leatherbound desk diary, sitting in on business meetings with our legs crossed at the ankle, taking down shorthand and then serving the coffee. And then after ten years or so of that privileged position, we might become a PERSONAL ASSISTANT to an even more important businessman, requiring us to travel with him to European hotels we have booked in advance, making sure he has the right papers for the right meeting and even going so far as to be asked to dinner with the other overweight, sweating businessmen he's meeting and asked to order wine from the Wine List. Then, at the end of a long night, stone-cold sober, ordering each of the six sozzled businessmen a taxi and making sure they get home to their European wives and multilingual children. Could we think of anything more EXCITING?

But such adventures start with Typewriting Level 1, Pitman 2000 Shorthand, Office Practice, Commercial German, A-level English, Accounting Basics, O-level Commerce and Principles of Export.

The tall girl with the electric typewriter is Faye Mortimer. She's older than us, nineteen, with a tumble of creamy hair and very tight jeans. She makes it plain at break time that she lived a life before she came back to college. She waitressed her way around California and surfed the golden sands of Santa Cruz before she ran out of money. She had love affairs and boyfriends and her own flat and even a driving licence but had to briefly move back in with her parents because she knew that her future lay forevermore in America and for that she needed some qualifications.

Three of us are sitting around the impossibly glamorous older woman. She offers round her cigarettes and we all take one. She even has her own lighter with her name engraved on the front.

'I'm here for the fucking certificates,' she says, 'not to learn how to give head.'

I say nothing because I have no idea what the last part of the sentence means but I too am here for the certificates, so I nod and cough on the strongest cigarette I have ever tasted. Jackie and Pam, my new friends, start in on Strick.

'She's missing the "t" off the end of her name,' says Jackie.

'Someone told me she's just got married, that's why she keeps playing with her wedding ring,' says Pam in horror. 'She looks about forty, for God's sake.'

Faye watches us, her eyes squinting against the smoke.

'Don't know about you lot but I'm never going to get through a fucking year of this.'

I'm jealous to the core of her cool loucheness, her easy way with the swears and her long-distance vision. I determine to part my hair down the middle and lose half a stone by next week. If I'm ever going to edge to the front of her magic circle, I'll need a cheesecloth blouse, a wristful of bangles and my own pack of cigarettes. She's wearing flip-flops with her jeans. Check. She's got tassels on her soft blue leather bag. Check. And her teeth, like Lorraine's, are slightly bucked. There's no way I can achieve that, not with my wide gap and big lips. And freckles are out. But I could at least work on my bad language.

We're all sitting near the back for Commercial German. Herr Fischer is exasperated with us. Three months in and we still can't order a boiled egg for our boss's breakfast. When he loses his temper, he spits on every 's'. I shield my face with my German textbook as he walks the rows spraying his instructions.

'Ssso. What is a boiled egg? Anyone?' He looks straight at me.

'*Ein gekochtes Ei.*'

'*Ja! Ja! Und so?*'

I speak quickly so he can move on. '*Ich hätte gern ein Doppelzimmer mit Bad für zwei Nächte und ein gekochtes Ei zum Frühstück.*'

'*Ja!* I would like a double room with bath for two nightsssss and a boiled egg for breakfasssst! Why is it that thisssss sssstudent can get it right and the resssst of you are sssso reluctant to try?'

Faye is doodling on the front of her exercise book. He shakes his head as he walks past.

'You know, girlsss, German is really a rather beautiful language, full of depthsss and nuance the English language, if you will forgive me, simply doesn't possesssss. Faye, are we boring you?'

Faye looks up.

'Faye, Faye, Faye,' he says, squeezing between the desk until he stands over her. 'With your, er, obvious maturity, I would have thought you would see the value in ssspeaking another language. You desire to travel, no?'

She says nothing. He bends from the waist until his face is level with hers.

'Exit,' he says.

'*Ausgang,*' she replies.

'Meeting.'

'*Treffen,*' she says, her eyes steady.

'Friendly,' he whispers.

'*Freundlich,*' she whispers back.

'Can you be *freundlich*, Faye?'

'*Sehr,*' she says, without missing a beat. 'I've been known to be very, very friendly. And I can also scratch like a cat.'

He straightens up slowly and walks to the front.

'Homework. Read the chapter on German customs and write down your order for a three-course meal for four people with wine. German wine!' he says as we scrape our chairs and squeeze out of the door.

We head for the refectory. I'm tight in Faye's group now. There are four of us, Jackie, Pam, Lynn and me. We find our favourite table near the Engineering apprentices' corner and light up. I'm smoking Faye's brand, Rothmans.

'What a fucking pervert,' she says. 'I could get him into trouble if I wanted.'

'I think that's what he wants to do with you,' I say and everyone laughs. Everyone except Faye.

'What are you doing after?'

'Me?'

'Yeah.'

'Fuck all,' I say, overjoyed to be singled out and to demonstrate my newfound prowess with profanity.

'Meet me after, I'll come into town with you.'

29

The Revolution

We sit upstairs on the bus and have two fags each. Faye tells me more about California and her golden life. She talks about guys, not boys, about scenes, not clubs or pubs. She calls her friends chicks and her enemies dogs. I shrug and nod and try to look like I've heard it all before.

'Why are you going into town?' I ask.

'You'll see.'

We get off the bus and head up New Street towards the Town Hall. There's a narrow little alley between a boarded-up shop and a second-hand jeweller's and she nips down there. I follow. In she goes through a green door with peeling paint and up some concrete stairs. Her bag swings, her hair swings, she knows where she's going.

As she walks, she shouts, 'Hey, hey!' Her voice echoes, bouncing off the brown painted walls, graffiti and smeared paint, cartoons and posters everywhere. She pushes through some wired glass doors and along a corridor.

'Hey, hey!'

It's freezing and musty but at the end of the long walk there's an open door and music playing. We walk towards it and into a big room with metal shelves everywhere like it was once an office or a library. The sun shines through dusty windows and on to a tall, white man, so thin his stomach is concave. He has the strangest hairstyle I have ever seen, shaved everywhere except the top, where bleached blond locks are piled up high, some ends escaping like white snakes lying on his neck. He has no eyebrows but strips of black eyeliner that match his leather trousers and leather vest. He's ironing a red silk shirt and singing along about a revolution that will not be televised.

Except he's not really singing, he's talking like a black man from an American cop show. He's reciting the song like a poem and every so often he stands the iron up and nods, points at me and nods again.

'Do you think the revolution will be televised?'

I don't know what to say so I drop my bag with my German homework and sit down on huge floor cushions covered with old carpet. I want to stare and look and look again, I want a few minutes to take it all in and swallow it down, bathe in the scene, in the sense that I'm somewhere exciting and different. Faye kisses the man and sits next to me. She puts a tin in my lap and drags the tendrils of her hair on top of her head, winding it round and round itself until it stays put.

'Go on,' she says.

I open the tin. There's a khaki sort of loose tobacco inside and some cigarette papers. I look back at her.

'Give it here,' she says, smiling, and she splits open a cigarette, empties the tobacco on to a paper and sprinkles in some of the khaki stuff. I'm not really watching because the man has finished with his silk shirt and is putting it on. He's so thin he's almost transparent and his leather trousers hang low on his narrow hips. He looks like a pop star in his red shirt. He's smiling at me with a massive mouthful of teeth and still talking along, singing along, putting his leather waistcoat back on over his shirt.

Faye passes me her new cigarette and pats her chest.

'Keep it down,' she says. 'The smoke, keep it down.'

It tastes half bitter, half sweet, and I close my eyes and concentrate on holding the warmth in my chest for as long as possible. When I breathe out, there's practically nothing there.

'Pass it to Max,' she says.

I pass it on and Max goes to the record player in the corner of the room and starts the same record all over again. He dances around with the sweet cigarette and and every time the song says, 'The revolution will not be televised,' we all say it together and we pass the sweetness and we sing and we hold the sweetness inside and we sing until we are all shouting together, '*The revolution will not be televised!*' and I start to laugh.

The laughter starts where I kept the smoke, deep in my chest, and radiates out from my throat to my fingers and toes and behind my eyes and up into the top of my head and paints everything white and light and happy.

Faye is watching me with half-open eyes. She's happy as well. And Max is putting on another record and beckoning me on to my feet. He pulls me up and starts doing a floaty dance.

'*Golden Years, gold, whop, whop, whop . . .*'

He's not embarrassed to be dancing like a girl in broad daylight in a dirty room with no curtains on the windows and a messy double bed in one corner of the room and empty bookcases and a fireplace that has no fire even though it's freezing cold and going dark. Faye is nodding her head and smiling.

And the next sweet cigarette has come round to me and I'm dancing with David Bowie and Max on a Tuesday night and the sun shines on the dusty windows and the world is a very, very nice place.

When it's really black outside, Faye walks me to the bus stop.

'You're OK,' she says. It's not a question and I suck it down where I kept the sweet, sweet smoke.

The 91 takes me right to the end of the street and when I get off I stay at the bus stop for a few minutes, checking myself over.

I've got my bag. Yeah. I've got my shoes on. Yeah. And my coat. Yeah. Coat. Yeah. And my hair. My hair is good. My hair is very tidy. I am very tidy. Stop laughing, because nothing is funny. Ha ha ha ha. Nothing is funny. Not one single thing. Check your hair. Hair is good. Not by the hair on your chinny chin chin. Why do people say pigs went to market and not a goat or chicken? And it was pigs that had their house blown down by the wolf. Is it the same pigs or different pigs? It's a shame for pigs. Stop laughing. I'm OK. I'm OK. Act natural. What's natural for fuck's sake? Walking is natural. All right, I'm home. I'm going to go inside and go upstairs. Straight upstairs. You're OK. You can do it.

The house is quiet. I remember it's Tuesday. Everyone has gone to the meeting. Dad is watching the telly.

'You late!' he shouts without moving his head.

'I went to my friend's house to revise,' I mutter as I climb the stairs. I lie on my bed under the window and watch the light of the passing bus on the ceiling above me. It starts in one corner then arcs to the other side of the room like searchlights in a prisoner-of-war film looking for the escapee. Run, run, climb the barbed wire. Head off across the grass. Don't get caught. You are free.

30

Who's Got the Map?

The best afro in college is owned by Mikey. He sits with the Engineering apprentices and wears a red check shirt and very well-pressed jeans. He notices me. I notice him. This has been going on for months. He's tall and skinny with a high bum and languid walk. He's not handsome, all his features are too big – his nose, his lips, his goldfish eyes – but he has beautiful hands. He holds a cigarette like Marlene Dietrich, like a God. He talks with his friends and glances over at me. He talks with his friends and leans his chair against the wall, balancing it at an engineer's angle, the perfect calibration of cool, safe and dangerous. Even when his classmates are laughing and joking, he never smiles. Just glances over and sometimes nods.

Faye says she's had enough. 'No way. He's one of them guys. All notes and no music.'

She hooks her fingers in her mouth and whistles. The whole canteen goes quiet. Everyone looks. He looks.

She gestures at me and points at him. 'Well? You gonna just sit there?' she shouts.

'Don't!' I hiss.

'What? He fancies you and you fancy him. What?'

He does nothing, doesn't even look embarrassed, but just as we're all going back to our classes, he sidles up to me.

'You're Mandy,' he says. 'I'm Mikey.'

'I know.'

He raises his eyebrows. 'That's the small talk done, then.'

Faye and the others hang back but I can hear them tittering.

'Your friend says you'd like to go out with me,' he says.

'She also said you're all notes and no music,' I reply, already at the limit of my banter.

We walk along the corridor until we have to go our separate ways.

'I'll meet you outside after,' he says. 'See if I can play you some tunes.'

'OK.'

'You get the 17, then the 8, then a bus along Stratford Road. You live down themways.'

'How do you know that?' I ask, but he's gone. His high, tight arse disappearing round the corner.

Faye and the others tease me for the rest of the afternoon. Faye asks if I'm on the pill and tells me to be careful. She tells me to play it cool and he's lucky to get within half a mile of someone as good-looking as I am.

'I mean,' she says, 'he's punching well above his weight. He's pretty ugly.' No one disagrees.

He's waiting for me outside the main gate and we get the bus together, sitting on top with our cigarettes. I wish I'd worn my best A-line corduroy skirt and not a dress with flowers on, but I had no idea I'd be sitting next to Superfro on my way into town.

He tells me all about myself, how his father knows my father, that they came over from St Kitts together. His father will be like my father, who knows all the Kittians that came over and whether they settled in Leeds or Manchester, what they do for a living and whether they ever made it back home. Mikey says he's asked people about me and knows I've got three sisters and a brother and an Irish mother. Says he's been watching me and likes what he sees. Likes my clothes and my hair and my wedge shoes. Likes the colour of my skin and the gap in my teeth. Likes the way I carry myself.

'You don't go on with slackness,' he says, and all this while he's looking straight ahead and not at me, as the bus wends through the narrow streets of South Yardley. He says everything like we're discussing a third person, like I might have an opinion on his research and say 'Well done' when he's finished.

We get off and walk the streets of the city centre, talking and looking in shop windows. We pass a girl laying into a cream cake, half of it in a paper bag, the other half in her mouth, and Mikey shakes his head.

'Don't walk and eat, man.'

I wonder if chewing gum counts and Polo mints, but I don't say anything. I watch the girl and wonder if everyone else thinks she's got bad manners. I didn't know about the 'Don't Walk and Eat' rule.

A black girl with big hoop earrings catches his eye.

'Nah, man. Don't smoke on the street.'

Mikey tells me more about his rules for optimum behaviour and his plans for the future. He works in the office of a foundry in Smethwick, he designs parts for machines that make other machines. He's the apprentice and gets the shit job, makes the tea sometimes, serves the other draughtsmen.

'Fuckers always taking the piss,' he says as we lean against the wall outside Virgin Records. 'But that job can't hold me. Mikey Douglas is better than that. Job can't hold me.'

This is a different breed of confidence to Max and Faye. I can feel the anger radiating off Mikey, the pride, the resentment.

'What are you going to do?' I ask.

'Get my own business. Get a handmade suit with a waistcoat from Angeli on Broad Street. Pinstripe. Get a Triumph Spitfire. Get a house in a good area. Get my own business. People can't hold Mikey.'

I notice now the perfection of him, the half-moon cuticles of his fingernails, the shine on his shoes and the symmetrical bows on the laces, the neatness of his belt and the smooth shine of his shave, the unbroken circumference of his fro. I notice his certainty and his dedication to his own salvation.

We walk around for ages until we end up near my bus stop. I go to walk across Martineau Square and he seems to hang back. We get to the alleyway that leads down to Bull Street and the bus terminus. He stops.

'Not going down there,' he says, gesturing to the steps.

'Why not?'

'You go down,' he says. 'Go on, go down the steps.'

'Why?'

'Just do it, you'll see.'

I've walked the steps before; there are only seven of them, wide steps made of paving stones. I get to the bottom and I turn round.

'Come back,' he says, so I do.

'See how they make you walk? Whoever made them steps designed them too wide. You can't go down one foot at a time. Halfway down you look like a cunt. At some point, you have to put your two foot on one step. Them steps make you walk funny. They do it on purpose to make a fool out of you.'

'What are you talking about?'

'You think they don't know what they're doing? They could have made the steps properly but they make them too wide to make you look stupid. I'm not going down the Cunt Steps.'

I'm laughing. He isn't.

'Nah, man, you think is joke? Watch.'

We watch everyone do the same thing and it's nothing. It's a half-step, the most insignificant little shuffle, and then you're down at the bottom. I'm laughing and looking at him.

'You're serious?'

'You didn't hear me? Walk down the Cunt Steps and they've won. Not me. I don't do them things. I know how them people think.'

'Who?' I ask. But I don't need the answer. It's the white man of my father's speeches, the people who won't give me a job, Mrs Kent, the police, people in charge.

When the bus comes, he touches me for the first time. A little shove on my shoulder. He tells me we're going to the pictures on Saturday night. Says he'll meet me outside at half seven, The Gaumont.

I don't say no.

It's Friday. It's exam season. I'm one of two girls taking 120-words-per-minute shorthand. Top in typing. A-level English, a breeze. I can complete Bills of Lading for Abu Dhabi, maintain a cash book for single-entry bookkeeping, get my boss to Munich by rail and make sure he gets a wake-up call at seven thirty, porridge at eight and a taxi at nine. All in German.

Faye was not wrong that the year would break us. Only spliffs and music have made it bearable. *Songs in the Key of Life*, Stevie Wonder's twenty-track double album, forms the backdrop of my life. I pick apart the lyrics and turn the words over and over, feeling the poetry on my tongue.

One Saturday I go into town and buy *Innervisions* from the record shop in town and dash home to the front-room gram and put it on. Me and Tracey sit cross-legged on the floor and pass the sleeve between us and listen until we can sing every chorus, until we can sing every verse, and I marvel at a blind man talking about the things that he can see, a milk-and-honey land. Does he know about Jehovah and Armageddon? 'Visions' is the one song I can't listen to when I'm stoned. It reminds me that I will die.

It's the last day of term. I'm waiting at the bus stop with Faye; we're going to see Max to say goodbye. Faye's going to London to wait for her exam results. Then Heathrow.

'Then it's *ciao* to the land of grey,' she says.

Max's squat has grown over time. There are people everywhere – Liz and G and Pippa and five or six students who never made it home after their degrees. Max still has his own room, but it's dirty and dark, and since they turned off the electric he's become the same colour as the big windows covered in sticky grime from the busy road below. He washes in a bowl in the corner of the room. His red silk shirt hangs by a nail, limp and threadbare.

'I know you won't fucking write, Faye,' he says, passing her the spliff, 'so don't even say you will. You didn't last time.'

'Yeah? You should try having the energy to do anything after eighteen hours on your feet, bar to diner, bar to diner, bar to diner.'

It's the first time her adventures have taken on the pallor of real life.

'And it's so expensive in San Francisco. I didn't eat some days. And Debbie turned out to be a bitch.'

'Could have told you that,' he says.

'Yeah, well. She took my bloke.' Faye forgets to pass the spliff on to me. 'And if I go back, I'm not even going to California. I've decided. New Mexico is where it's at.'

The 'if' sounds like thunder. She looks up suddenly. The cat is creeping out of the bag. She snaps it shut.

'I mean, it was great and everything. I'm still going. Definitely. Yeah. But just to New Mexico, that's all.'

She finally hands me the spliff and puts on a record. She starts swaying and singing. We smoke some more, play another few records, and I leave early. I kiss Faye goodbye.

I won't see Max without her. It's become too grim, too sad. The room is too cold and too dirty.

'You're all right,' she says and holds me for a long time. 'I'll write.'

'Yeah, and I'll write back,' I say.

She tucks her weed tin in my hand. 'Look after yourself.'

I smoke the last two inches of my last spliff as I walk the long way to the bus stop through the Bull Ring and down to St Martin's Church. I saunter past the bus station and up Bradford Street, cut into the tower blocks of Highgate and into Moseley Village. It's miles and miles, and I don't care. I don't notice. I'm eking out the spliff, letting it go out and lighting it again. The trees are an impossible green and the sun paints everything gold and bright. It's seven o'clock and it's Friday and I've finished college and, by the weight of it, Faye's weed tin is half full.

Mikey didn't last long. The rules were legion and I couldn't keep up. I was always going to be less than his vision of me. But there's a pretty-looking mixed-race waiter in one of the hotels in town who always gives me the eye when I walk past. I think about him and his big eyes and crooked smile, and wonder how to get past the mutual-adoration stage. And there's a weird-looking white boy who works in the bacon shop on Stratford Road. He has a limp, a very bad haircut and dark-blue eyes.

I wonder about blue eyes and brown eyes and black boys and white boys, and feel the whole world expand before me like a golden road that leads ever onward.

I'm thirsty when I get home. I walk into the kitchen to get some water but immediately stop at the door. Dad is there. He's sitting at the kitchen table. And Mom is sitting next to him. And Tracey is sitting next to them both.

I am absolutely stoned to fuck and I am presented with something I have seen possibly twice in my life: Mom and Dad sitting down, close, next to each other, at the same table. Tracey's presence levels it up from unusual to surreal. What's going on? The only explanation is that the table scene is normal and I am not. The paranoia kicks in hard and deep. What do I do? Can I leave the room? If I turn on the tap and fill a cup with water, is that a normal thing to do? Will it look weird? Do I even live here?

I walk to the sink and stop. I turn round. They are looking at me. It feels like a soft interrogation session by the SS. The one where they pretend to be friendly and take you out to dinner. After a few glasses of wine, they start asking you questions to see if your backstory checks out.

'Ah, Regensburg! Bavaria! *Ja!* There is a beautiful bridge there, *nein?*'

But the spy doesn't know if there's a bridge there or not because he comes from Tunbridge Wells, only his mother was half-Swiss so he learned German from her and got sent behind enemy lines after spending six weeks being shown how to take photographs with a fountain pen . . . Where am I? I try to pull back from the rest of the story. There's nothing else I can do but sit down and let the questions begin.

Dad: College done?
Stoner: Yes, Dad.
Mom: No more three buses there and three buses back.

Stoner: No. Yes.

[*Tracey's eyes are twinkling. She knows.*]

Tracey: Where have you been?

Stoner: Where have I been?

Tracey: Yes. Where. Have. You. Been?

Stoner: Walking home.

Dad: From where?

Stoner: I can't remember.

[*Tracey laughs and turns it into a cough.*]

Stoner: Er, I mean, I lost my bus fare.

Dad: You hungry?

Stoner: No. I went to my friend's house.

Dad: What they give you?

Stoner: Cabbage.

[*The vegetable appears from nowhere. Tracey is biting the inside of her cheek. Her eyes are watering.*]

Dad: Cabbage? Cabbage? Cabbage and what?

Stoner: [*Think, goddamit. Think.*] Egg.

Tracey: Cabbage and egg?

[*Whose side is she on? We won't win the war like this.*]

Dad: Who eat cabbage and egg? What kind of people is this? Cabbage and egg? Where they come from? Sound like Polish people food, eh, Sheilo?

Mom: Is she Polish?

Stoner: Who?

Mom: The girl?

What fucking girl? What's gone wrong? Who's got the map?

Tracey, God bless every atom of her, takes pity. She gets

up and takes my bag from where it has been sitting on my lap like a shield between me and the Gestapo.

'We're going to play some records,' she says to Mom and Dad, and lifts me by the arm, shoves me into the front room and laughs like a drain.

31

Lion of Judah

Kim is first to leave home. She's been listening carefully at the Kingdom Hall and when Brother Stannard said that the need was great in the north-east and he described the desperation of the small congregations in Sunderland and Newcastle that have to preach the good news of the Kingdom to hundreds of square miles of rural towns and villages, she takes it to heart.

Kim packs her bags and says goodbye. She sends us letters from Durham and perfect ink drawings of a terraced street in Ushaw Moor where she lives in a one-up-one-down house with a real fire and outside yard. She preaches to miners' families, she cleans the big houses of university professors, she reasons with anthropologists and scientists about the seven days of creation and disproves transubstantiation with the trainee priests in the Catholic seminary. She's doing God's work and our mother can hold her head up at the meetings. One of her daughters is doing the right thing at least.

Me and Tracey have more or less stopped going to the meetings, finding excuse after excuse on Tuesdays and Thursdays, oversleeping on Sundays. Mom stands over us in our beds and cries about it.

'Why can't you be more like Kim? What's going to become of you when Armageddon comes?'

I keep my eyes closed.

'Oh, Jehovah!' she says, raising her eyes to the ceiling. 'Help them understand!'

No lightning bolt breaks through the roof. No angel appears at the end of the bed. The end of days, 1975, was two years ago. It has come and gone and the tower blocks didn't topple into the mouth of the earthquake. The baddies are still running the world, and me and Tracey are still smoking cheap cigarettes and filching coins out of Dad's trouser pockets while he sleeps. Jehovah's Witnesses got their sums wrong and we know it.

Instead, we put our faith in Bob Marley, Peter Tosh, Dennis Brown and Burning Spear. We sit cross-legged with our ear to the gram in the front room, singing along in the new Jamaican accents we are cultivating from the lyrics. Mom is red-eyed and worn down by our lack of faith and refusal to go to the meetings for more indoctrination. She drags Dean and Karen with her three times a week with renewed zeal while saving up in earnest to go back to America, to get away from us, to get away from Dad.

She books herself another Miami flight to leave just before Christmas.

'I need some sun,' she says with a sniff, making sure Dad can hear. 'It'll be nice and hot in Key West.'

She packs the same suitcase with the same clothes and takes a taxi to the coach station for the journey to Heathrow.

'Bye, Mom!' we shout from the front door. Tracey and I look at one another, her departure fitting perfectly into our plans. She's gone for three months this time and by the time she comes back we are living in Handsworth in a rented house with lino in the front room and two mattresses on the floorboards upstairs.

I stop temping in the banks and offices of the city centre and sign on the dole. Tracey's money and mine is just about enough to live on if we don't pay the gas bill and hardly eat. The bulk of it goes on weed and what's left buys coffee, milk and records.

We lose weight, we gain friends, we reason into the early hours of the morning, learning about Haile Selassie and Marcus Garvey's fleet of Black Star liners. We spend our nights in blues and shebeens, our days asleep. I become a master spliff builder, finding a simple, engrossing beauty in their construction, the perfect tip, the flat end with the tiny little twist of Rizla. There is not a day when I am not completely and magnificently stoned.

One day, there is a knock on the door. It's mid-afternoon so we are awake. It's Kim. We hug and she steps inside and tells us about her ministry and the loneliness of Durham, how one day she woke up and knew she had to come home. She looks around at our bare house and our bare white walls.

'Are there any shops round here?' she says.

'Top of the road. Why?'

She walks out and comes back with a set of paints and a paintbrush, and while we talk and smoke and drink sweet tea, she starts. She paints freehand, doesn't ask us what we think or what we want. She makes a map of Africa and a black woman and a slave and a Rasta man, and the river that would take us back across the water to whatever African country we were stolen from, and the Lion of Judah, and when she's finished, we know she has left the Witnesses for good. She has lost the same thing we all have.

The next day, we all go home to Springfield Road. Mom is at work and Dad is in the telly room. Karen's in the kitchen, a teenager now and alone with the two of them since Dean moved out to live with his girlfriend and make music in the wild depths of Balsall Heath.

'We have to move out of our house, Karen,' I say. 'I'll be moving back into Moseley. I think Tracey's moving in with her friend. I'll be closer to you and we can—'

Dad shuffles into the kitchen in his slippers. He's aged suddenly, his hair grey, a slovenly look about him. His shirt isn't ironed, he's become jowly and heavy-lidded. He's wearing slippers, not Italian leather Chelsea boots, not a mohair suit or a shirt-jack in midnight linen. All the things he bought to wear in St Kitts are tucked away upstairs, unworn, unneeded.

'Put the kettle on,' Karen says to him, her voice flat and commanding. I stare at her, open-mouthed. I'm waiting for Dad to turn round and say, 'Who you think you is talking to?' but instead he picks up the kettle, fills it with water and turns the gas on.

'We need some biscuits, don't we?' she says to me but looks at Dad.

'You want money for biscuits?' he says. 'Here,' and digs into his baggy trousers for change. 'Run down the shops, get some.'

I take the money with wide eyes and when we are on the street I look hard at Karen's face.

'Did you really just give Dad an order?'

She smiles. 'He's all right with me,' she says. 'He spent all his anger on you lot. There's nothing left.'

He's made the tea by the time we get home. He sits in the kitchen with us for a while and makes small talk about the television, about the government, but asks no questions until the conversation dwindles to nothing. He stands up and shuffles back to the telly room and *The Streets of San Francisco*.

32

Everybody Becomes Somebody

Madame Symanski rents out every spare room in her enormous Victorian villa in Moseley Village. Number 34 Beauchamp Hill is beautiful and shabby with exotic spiky weeds in the garden and lavish plumes of white wisteria falling over the front door. The house smells of pickles, mould and a pale-pink meat she cooks with lemon and onions on Sunday afternoons. I have a bedsit at the front of the house, an enormous mucus-coloured room with a dark wood floor and plasterwork yellowed by damp from some ancient and persistent leak. There's a kitchen at the back with a two-ring burner and cast-iron sink with an uneven mosaic floor that would overlook the garden if Symanski hadn't permanently misted over the glass.

Madame lives in part of the first floor with her silent bearded husband and the seven-year-old Aleksandra, who is so pretty that when she passes it's impossible not to stare, and she stares back, meets you full and frank with hard blue eyes that never seem to blink.

The main hall downstairs houses the bathroom shared between the three ground-floor flats. It's really just a cupboard under the wide staircase, no toilet but an almost bottomless white stone tub that looks like a sheep dip with a little seat halfway down so you don't drown while you sit in tepid water in the murky light and wait for Madame Symanski to rattle the door handle and tell you 'Time is up!'

There's a huge basement that spans the width of the house where she tends the ship's boiler that services the ten rooms of number 34. There are no radiators in the downstairs rooms for her unemployed lodgers but occasionally warm, fetid air wafts up through black metal grilles set into the floorboards. It happens without warning and only sometimes. It might be that she hears me sneezing or the thermometer tells her that I might die of hypothermia or she needs to cool the boiler down, but every so often I hear her clopping down the concrete steps to the cellar and fiddling with the winding handle of the contraption that opens the grille to my room. I hear it rattle and scrape and, when I look down, I see her looking up at me from the darkness, her thin smile, her narrow eyes and a nod.

'It is cold,' she throws at me as though it might be news.

'Thank you,' I reply as I stand over the grille and feel my feet come back to life.

Upstairs, above me, lives Christian. He's an ex-student who never made it back home after his anthropology degree at Birmingham University. His degree remains unused and unemployed. He wears a huge black trench coat with dull brass buttons and Dr Martens. Everything is too big for him – his clothes, his ideas, the world in general.

He walks his room all night, talking to himself, singing to himself, and Madame Symanski has to bang on his door and tell him to go to bed. Sometimes, he makes strange vegetarian balls of sticky brown rice that he places in some kind of mysterious pattern on a golden tray. He knocks everyone's door and makes us take a particular one.

'That one is yours because I put essence of Boswellia in it for posture. You're bending wrong.'

'Yeah, thanks, Christian,' I say, careful to close the door before he can come inside. Once, he didn't leave for two days and talked non-stop. He never went for a piss in all that time.

He's kind to the point of stupidity, lends his money to the village scroungers, helps us to catch moths and mice, balancing his six foot three inches on a saucepan or splintered chair, holds the door for us, comes home with Turkish Delight for Mr Symanski and learns Polish nursery rhymes for Aleksandra. He always, always, always asks how you are and waits for an answer. And he is completely mad.

Every so often he goes home to his parents somewhere in Staffordshire and returns laden with food and money and gifts and clothes that he owns for exactly five minutes before his new friends, the thieving chancers of Moseley Village, come round and clean him out.

I'm leaving the sheep dip one day when I hear the front door open. I'm freezing. I'm boiling. I'm getting some kind of fever yet all I want to do is get hotter and hotter. I don't have a hot-water bottle and I don't have any money to buy one. I've smoked my last bit of weed and can't face the journey to Sandford Road to get some more. I have no milk.

I hear footsteps in the hallway and a cough. With Madame Symanski and Aleksandra banging around upstairs, I know it's either Christian, Symanski senior or my brother, who rents the room opposite. I pull the towel tight and peek round the corner. If it's Dean, I can ask him to lend me a fiver or make me some toast or just make him feel sorry for me. But I'm not peeky enough and there he is, smiling like a Mormon. Christian.

'Yeah, yeah, I had a bath this morning but the water started running cold,' he says, taking two giant steps towards me. He always starts midway through a conversation we haven't been having. I half trot to my room, my wet feet slipping on the ice-cold floor tiles. My damp T-shirt, my bra and knickers drop from my arms and I bend down to pick them up, still bunching a knot of thin, soaking towel in my fist. Not that I couldn't let it drop and stand there buck naked while he talked. Christian is unstoppable.

'Yeah, yeah, and then, yeah, went into the village . . .' He pushes open the door to my room and I scamper in. He leans on the door jamb, 'There you go, yeah.'

He's almost in the room now, carrying on without a pause. 'Saw Hughie just now, yeah, yeah. He's lost all his fucking gear, man. Robbed when he was sort of . . . you know Hughie. Anyway, Church Road or somewhere, yeah, I couldn't see him like that. Sort of pained me here.' He taps his chest where his big heart lives. 'Gave him my coat and keffiyeh and I had that scarf since I was in Palestine. I mean, yeah. But you know, I sort of had to.'

'Hughie? Fucking hell, you're an idiot, Christian,' I say, trying to close the door.

'Ah, yeah, I mean, yeah,' he says with his angelic face and watery eyes, 'it's my destiny. So, yeah, you know, me and you have talked about this before, yeah. Hughie needing the coat was like pretty much unavoidable and my giving it to him was unavoidable. If you—'

'Yeah, destiny, destiny. I remember. OK. Doesn't mean you've got to let people shit on you, Christian. You can still say no. And can you just . . .' I ease the door towards him. He smiles and shakes his head.

'She was always angry,' he whispers and backs away slowly. 'Turmoil.' In two strides he is halfway up the stairs. I watch him go, his jeans hanging off his backside, his jumper, mostly holes, covering the sharp bones of his back.

'What?'

He jumps over the banister and is in my room before I can move.

'Jezebel,' he says, folding his legs under him like a praying mantis as he concertinas down on to my floor cushions.

'Fucking hell, Christian.' I close the door and pull the blanket off my bed, hunching under it to get dressed. He politely looks away but keeps going.

'Yeah, yeah, she was in turmoil, that's what people didn't realize. Turmoil, yeah? People don't realize that her . . . her . . . ways, yeah, the way she behaved, was because she was angry and lost. She was you, yeah, yeah. You and her,' he says, knitting his hands together and showing me the evidence.

'Oh, I'm Jezebel?'

'Was, was.'

I stand over him, dripping hair, hands on still-damp hips. 'Don't tell me, Christian, reincarnation?'

He nods with his eyes closed. 'Yeah, yeah, she has passed to you.'

'And you've met her, like, when you were back there in biblical times?'

'Throughout, yeah.'

'Oh, right. Who were you then? John the Baptist?'

'Joseph of Arimathea,' he says, like he's giving his name to the dole office. 'Yeah, yeah. Had to step in and help with the burial of Christ. It was a day like today, actually. Chilly.'

I've been here before with Christian. He's bored me through every era from the Dark Ages to post-war Germany and his significant part in the liberation of Berlin. I'm too ill to pretend I'm swallowing any of it.

'Oh yeah,' I say, 'I remember you telling me about that time you held the door for Henry the Eighth as he walked through Hampton Court with his new wife. Which one was it again?'

'Anne.'

'Cleeves?'

'Boleyn.'

'Of course it was,' I say, touching my forehead. He looks up while I pace to and fro, five steps, wall to wall, trying to get warm. 'That's the thing about reincarnation, isn't it, Christian? Everybody is somebody.'

'Yeah, yeah, that's right,' he says, smiling, happy to have finally converted me. 'Everyone *becomes* somebody.'

'No, what I mean is, everyone is a queen, a courtier, Michael Angelo's chisel maker, Da Vinci's sister, Shakespeare's scribe. Can't remember the last time I heard one of you lot say, "Oh yeah, I was a pervert who killed a girl in the Middle Ages." Yeah? Or, "I was a village idiot with no teeth, can't remember much about it because I only had an

IQ of forty-eight." Or, "I was a farmer from the scrublands of Westphalia and I did nothing and every day was the same, brought in the hay, fed the pigs, died in my sleep." No action, no news whatsoever. No. You're all a big some-one or knew the big someone or did the big something.'

He looks away, examines his fingernails. I can't help but go on, the fever eating away at my patience and good manners.

'It's just another way of being special, Christian. You're no different from the Jehovah's Witnesses. "Oh, God only loves us. Just us. We're the chosen ones. We will be in paradise, you won't."'

I feel the rage of my childhood breaking through the water like a killer whale.

'And it would have been fucking grim to be alive in those days, Christian, and you'd be dead at thirty and not one iota like the Technicolor fucking MGM films on the telly, but no, it was all exciting, wasn't it? Just like now but better. Obviously. You want to think you were court jester for Henry the Eighth because you've got nothing going on in your life except being suckered by Hughie "Skank Arse" Miller.'

He runs his tongue around his gums then slowly levers himself up. He towers over me.

'Sorry,' he says, but like it's me he's sorry for, not him-self. He puts his hand on my shoulder and closes the door quietly afterwards.

I collapse on to the cushions, cocoon myself in the blanket and fall asleep.

*

I come to and the world is black. The ancient velvet curtains are wide open, rain thrums hard against the glass. It takes me five minutes to sit up and realize I'm properly sick. I can't face the chilly sheets of my bed, they might tip me over the edge. I have to stay where I am and wait it out.

I cover my feet and draw everything tight around me, arms, cushions, blankets, fortitude. I think about the noise and chaos of Springfield Road, how Mom would have made me a hot-water bottle and told everyone to shut up, Tracey would have sat on my bed and talked about music and the gossip of the street, Kim would have sat quietly, nose in book, and Dean and Karen and Dad would be milling around, running into my bedroom, running out again, and there'd be arguments and jokes and the wail of country music and the muffled rumble of *News at Ten* and smells of frying food, and I might wander down to the telly room and Dad would tell me to sit quiet and *Brief Encounter* might be on and I'd stand on the platform with Celia Johnson for the thousandth time and watch the train pull away.

I wake again to a knock on my door. I wonder if it's Symanski asking for the rent I don't have. It comes once more, a soft knock, and then the turn of the handle and it's Christian again. I see him at forty-five degrees. He crouches down and puts his hand on my forehead.

'Yeah, yeah, thought so,' then he's gone again but only for a moment. He comes back into the room with his golden tray and puts it down on the floor. He sits me up and pours frothing, herby tea from a small brass teapot with a bone handle.

'Hot, hot,' he cautions and makes little blowing noises like a mother to a child.

It tastes of nothing but sugar and kindness. It's all I can do not to cry.

'Yeah, yeah, you're not, you know, being yourself these days,' he says. 'Your shadow frequency is blocked.'

I sniff and sip.

'Your root chakra asks only one thing. Do I belong here?' he says.

'I don't know if I do, Christian.'

It becomes a lullaby, the chi, the muladhara, the mool, flow, awakening, earthing, on and on, hot tea, the light of Christian's candle on the golden tray and his long fingers moving in the air, sewing everything together. He tells me about dreams and déjà vu, how you meet people in another plane and then find their soul in the physical world; he tells me about reading tea leaves and palms, about sound baths and the mysteries of indigo, and so he goes on until he's covering me over with another blanket and placing his hand on my head.

Christian comes down the next day and the day after. He makes the tea in my kitchen and sits up reading and talking while I sleep. He won't buy me any weed, says it's bad for me, but instead lets me puff a bitter leaf on his hookah. I feel better on the third day and his stream of consciousness begins to grate.

'I'm going to see my sister,' I say when he lets himself in that evening. I've got my coat on and a duffle bag on my shoulder. I see him start. 'Oh, oh, yeah, I mean, yeah. I'll walk you to the bus stop, you know—'

'No, it's only on Sandford Road . . .'

He opens the front door for me, waves when I turn. I float back in the small hours as it's getting light, stoned to beggary, and sleep all the next day. I don't see Christian for weeks afterwards. He's gone home to Staffordshire for grounding and a financial top-up. Weeks spill into months and Symanski eventually puts all his things into a cardboard box and lets his room to a middle-aged boozer called Leo who has taken a religious vow to wear only red.

I'm in The Fighting Cocks in the village when I hear the news. I swallow hard, push through the crowd to the back door and lean against the wall. I'm stoned as fuck as usual and it takes ages to process that Christian is dead. Hanged himself in his mother's house. Left a note telling her she shouldn't worry. Death is just a temporary thing. He'd be back.

I roll myself a spectacular, five-Rizla spliff and suck on it all the way home. I sit on my cushions with shaking hands and listen to the noises in the house, the Symanski television, the grinding gears of the subterranean boiler, a scratchy noise behind the skirting boards and red footsteps above that no longer belong to my friend. I hear a moth against the window, but when I turn it stops suddenly, its fat brown belly hard on the glass. I wonder for a moment if it's Christian maybe, saying goodbye, and then I remember the scriptures that tell me that it can't be, that he's dead without hearing my thanks and gratitude, a kind soul, gone for good.

33

You Think You is the Only One?

For two years, my days don't change. I follow a pattern of afternoon waking, getting stoned, listening to music, signing on in Moseley Village, cashing my giro, feeling momentarily flush, buying weed, looking at the sky, listening to bands in The Fighting Cocks, talking. More talking. There are riots all over England so there's plenty to say and plenty to hear. Friends are arrested, friends are sectioned, friends are beaten in police cells, friends skip town. The police patrol the streets and arrest anyone they please. My friends go on demonstrations and sign petitions. I make placards but never actually get to the event. Sus laws are putting innocent black people behind bars, police brutality is the norm and we watch, unsurprised, as months of frustration and resistance overspill into the streets but gets reported as opportunistic hooliganism by the newspapers. We are angry. We are impotent.

I meet Pablo through a sort of boyfriend, Skip. It's summer and the heat has risen to Skip's attic flat in Handsworth. All the windows are open and everywhere, up the road and down, people are playing roots and rockers with the occasional slice of lovers' rock for flavour. The bass echoes all over the street so pure and sweet that we turn off our Barrington Levy and let next-door's Leroy Smart tell us 'Jah is My Light'. We're playing draughts on a piece of painted plywood, skipping the counters over the board, smoking and laughing. The door opens and a white man steps inside followed by a black woman who is dressed in African robes, vines of grey locks curled up around her head. She's easily six foot tall.

'Yo, yo, yo!' shouts Skip and as he stands on unsteady legs the board tips over and the game is done. 'You reach!

They all embrace, hard. 'Come, come,' says Skip, 'sit, man! Long time.'

'True,' says Pablo and I expect him to be one of those white men who speak patois, all the right words, all the right music, with the wrong accent. But Pablo just sits there in a Geography teacher's corduroy jacket, red jeans and office shoes. He takes out an old man's pipe, fills it with weed and talks like a newsreader, every word clear, good English, deep and strong. The black woman says nothing.

'When you come back?' says Skip.

'About four weeks ago,' he says and passes me the pipe with a nod. 'We had engagements in London.'

'Seen, seen. Mandy, man, this is Madura, my cousin. And this my spar, Pablo. We meet in Winson Green, share a cell seven months.'

'Nine, I think,' says Pablo, 'if you count the extra weeks.'

They start laughing and Skip tells me that Pablo spent two months on the run, living in this same flat, sleeping on the floor until the police found out where he was. The conversation turns to the riots and the state of the country. Pablo's political nous is startling. I only know about the obvious stuff, police brutality and racism; he has a wider grasp.

After a long monologue that takes in apartheid, colonialism, Keynesian economics, the transatlantic slave trade, communism, reparation and Orientalism, he takes a pause and then begins again. 'It's a question of ownership and agency,' he says, but Madura cuts him off.

She speaks like a man, like the men I heard on the platform at the Kingdom Hall, unapologetic, confident, scripture after scripture, except these scriptures come from her heart. She looks at us all, slowly, from one to the other, says a few words to each of us and then moves on, the light glinting off her two gold teeth, her bangles clinking together every time she raises her hand.

'What you think they want, these police, these politician? You think them want we in prison? How much prison cost? For each man to eat and stay warm and read his book by electric lighting, how much prison officer get pay, you know how much it cost to have doctor on call and take the man them to court in a black van? How much it cost judge and jury? What about police? How much you think it cost?'

It's not a question.

'You think Thatcher want to spend money on we, even money to lock we up? She don't instead want to take all fifteen thousand pounds it cost to keep each man in prison and give it to the army for them to go take land off another black man in Africa, in Iraq somewhere? She don't want we in prison! She want us out of the country, off the face of the earth. Or she want us cleaning the white man's toilets and bringing home little money to feed ourselves. And when she done with we, send us back! Mek dem go home! Yes! We finish with them now the country is on its feet, we finish with the black man. She want us doing jobs white men don't do so the white man can flourish. And then what? You think Thatcher want slavery done?'

She takes the pipe and we are all quiet while she thinks.

'A riot is part of a political process,' she says, settling back on the sofa. She's speaks softer now, smooth as velvet, seductive. 'You don't finish with riot. Before riot you have agitation, before agitation you have complaint, before complaint you have oppression. You have to look at history. Riot don't come from nowhere. But riot is only a part of a process. A bigger process. What comes after riot? That is the question.'

She goes on. Pablo goes on. I don't have the vocabulary for what I feel, the hurt of my people, the anger and confusion, but underneath it all, strongest of all, is the fear of this kind of certainty, this iron-strong doctrine, speeches like these that move me in my secret spiritual self but leave me feeling bad and not good enough, lacking conviction, that I should be doing more, thinking differently, thinking better. I wonder about the in-between world, the vast grey steppes, where doubts multiply and worry flourishes, where I live without answers. So I fall into the role of seeker of truth and ask questions – why, how, when – and swallow down the answers for later when I'm home alone and I can pick over the bones and make a meal of it all.

Red-eyed Pablo nods, fills the pipe, passes the pipe, and the sun sets. We share a few inches of brandy in a little glass and eventually they get up to leave. I see Skip take Pablo to one side.

'You good?' he asks him. He's inches from his face, scanning it for something.

Pablo nods.

'Me ask you if you is good, Pablo,' Skip says again.

'Really, I am. Yes,' says Pablo. 'Clean.'

Madura kisses me and calls me sister. 'One love,' she says and then they're gone.

A few months later I see Pablo coming out of the chemist in Moseley Village. He looks different, tired maybe.

'Ah,' he says, 'I met you at Skip's, right? How is he?'

'Good, I think, I don't see him any more. How is . . .?'

'Madura? She's touring, speaking. She's opened the Black Women's Collective. It takes up all her time, I'm afraid.' We're walking downhill towards the park.

'I think I may have held her back,' he said. 'We met when we were children. I'm Jamaican.'

I turn to take a better look. White people from Jamaica aren't unusual but the voice is. He smiles. 'My father sent me to England to be educated. Boarding school, Oxford, that sort of thing. Trying to wash out the black blood methinks.'

We sit on concrete steps by the outdoor theatre where a girl strums a guitar for fifty people. I light a spliff and pass it to him but he takes out one of his own. He pulls heavy on it, coughing discreetly into his hand.

'My new place is damp,' he says. 'Or I'm dying of old age.' He gives me a weak, sideways smile. 'I'm thirty next week.'

He looks older. He looks like a shipwrecked man who's lived under a burning sun, a man who's been rescued, washed and dressed, but under the clothes the damage remains.

'Youth is full of pleasance,' he says, 'age is full of care. That's Shakespeare but it could be Leonard Cohen. It's difficult to know the difference these days.'

The singing girl isn't very good. She's wordy and melancholy and I'm swept by a feeling of sadness for her and wonder why she's putting herself through it. The day isn't warm enough to sit outside, not really, and I'm only here because I met someone I hardly know and followed him. I look from one person to the next and realize no one is listening and nobody cares about the girl's troubles. When the drizzle starts, we wander into the arts centre and Pablo buys me a drink.

He starts mid-sentence.

'That's what happened in Kashmir, you learn you need very little, actually. Took me three years to learn that. Came home. We all come home.'

He carries on and I realize he thinks he's told me the first half of the story, something about losing everything and living off his wits, his father refusing to send him the money to come home.

'I learned to speak fluent Kashmiri. It does me no good here.'

He starts speaking in a language which sounds beautiful and strange on his tongue. It peters out after a few minutes.

KIT DE WAAL

'It's a story about a fish and a bridge. I forget the rest.'

As it grows darker, friends arrive from the village, singers and poets, artists, dossers, three of the 'we only wear red' brigade, one Hare Krishna, a white Rasta, and we spill on to the grass and into the arena for the rest of night. I smoke some excellent Lebanese black with a guy with too many teeth who makes me laugh and we dribble home to my flat for a few days until his stash has disappeared.

I see Pablo from time to time in pubs, at gigs, at parties, slipping into Moseley life and growing shabby. He loses weight and his teacher's wardrobe. He shaves his head badly and the cuts get infected. His hands are filthy and when we speak I can smell him, sour, sweaty, a vague note of shit.

One night in The Fighting Cocks, I see he's lost some teeth and his face is bruised under the dirt. I feel a lump of sorrow grow in my chest for the man I met on a summer's night, when music was playing and when I listened to a queen and learned something new about the world. I feel a lump of sorrow in my throat for Christian and for the mother who found him and for the golden tray I didn't rescue from Symanski. I feel the lump grow spikes that prickle my skin and make me shudder inside. I can't seem to breathe.

'You wouldn't happen to have a few pounds, would you?' he asks, spittle flying from his mouth.

'Sorry, Pablo, no, I don't. I'll buy you a drink,' I say.

'Can I have the money instead?'

It's such a bald and desperate ask, I give him some coins in spite of myself and he shuffles away. I see him sidle up to someone else, who shakes his head. And again. And again, until he's lost in the crowd.

'Junked-up chancer,' says my friend.

I'm walking down Strensham Hill to a lock-in at The Black Eagle. I'd rather not, but I've been swept along somehow and don't know how to leave. These are not my friends, just people I know. Just people I smoke with, drink with. I feel like if I go to The Black Eagle, something bad might happen. I'm not even stoned. I'm anxious. I'm tired.

It's been happening more and more every day, me staring into space and wondering about the movement of time and the machinations of my brain and whether I'm real and who is the other voice in my head and what actually is matter and where does space end, and on and on until my heart starts to hammer and I stand up suddenly and feel like I want to run away from myself.

And anyway, I know the conversations I'll have in The Black Eagle. I know them before they begin. Bands and guitars and gigs and drugs and Maggie Thatcher and the fucking police and my damp flat and your damp flat and rats and mice and sharing a kitchen and sharing a toilet and that girl who got arrested and that guy who went on the game and can you lend me a fiver and have you got a fag and when does your dole come and ashanti yoga and vegetarian shoes. And if I go with them and have to do this dance again, I'll be locked in The Black Eagle and I might go mad.

We are waiting to cross over the road when I see Pablo shuffling along. He's looking for cigarettes on the pavement and kicking at things in the gutter. I feel something slip inside. He walks past me without looking up and I watch him go. He walks down Park Road and up to the door of a big, old house everyone knows as a squat and pushes it open. I follow.

'See you there later!' I shout to my non-friends.

The door opens easily and I walk inside. It's the same smell of shit and filth that's layered on Pablo. There are papers and bottles in the hallway and vague murmurs coming from some of the rooms like it's the end of a party. I walk through, no one stops me. Everywhere, the innards of the house spill out like there's been a bomb or the walls have had a good kicking, paint, wallpaper, plaster, brick, pipes. In the kitchen, there's an old sofa with its guts ripped out and on that sofa is Pablo, picking the scab on his face.

'Pablo, you OK?' I say. He doesn't look up.

'No,' he says. 'She's really sick.'

'Who?'

He gets up and goes into a small room at the very back of the house. It's darker still, the air thick with something decaying, fetid like the breath of a hundred tramps, a hundred Mr Morgans. There, lying on a mattress under a blanket, is a woman with dirty, sour-cream hair, slightly bucked teeth and freckles. She's skinnier and paler and her skin is a type of yellow-green but she's still Faye.

I kneel down and take her hand because I can see she doesn't recognize me.

'Faye, Faye, remember me? It's Mandy. Garretts Green College. Typing. German.'

'Mandy,' she says, but her eyes are closed.

'Mandy,' I repeat. 'You were going to America. Remember?'

'Mandy,' she says. She half turns and her eyes flicker open. 'Yeah. Nice handwriting.'

'Yes, me.'

Then she turns back to the wall and pulls the blanket over her face.

'What's wrong with her?' I ask Pablo.

'I'm taking her to the doctor tomorrow,' he says quickly. 'I'm going to insist this time.'

'I said what's fucking wrong with her?'

'It's cold. Pretty difficult keeping this room warm in actual fact.'

I stand up. I back away bit by bit, looking at the narrow body under the blanket, the filth, the girl gone, the thing in her place. Pablo follows me out of the room.

'Have you got a fiver?' he asks and I shake my head.

'Fuck off.'

On the way home I see a dog dart down an alleyway. At another corner, a cat drops silently off a brick wall and slinks away. There are noises behind hedges and shadows on the pavement; leaves skitter across the road for no reason. Everything is very loud: the wind in the trees, cars driving past, a call somewhere, an answer. I am petrified.

By the time I open the door to my flat I'm breathing so hard my chest hurts. I can hear the tiniest noise, the creak of a floorboard, the rain on the window. All my senses are on high alert. I put my hands over my ears but the sounds inside are even worse. There's a sort of loud humming, a buzzing like there's a fly trying to escape, and I wonder if it's Christian.

I open the curtains and throw the blankets off the bed because if I can't find the fly I can't help him come back as a human.

I go back into the street, but it's too dark for flies. A man walks past on the other side of the road. I can hear his thoughts. He's thinking about selfish people who won't give money to dying friends so I run back inside and draw the curtains.

All I can do is wait for morning. My legs are shaking, my right one in particular. I put my hand on it, but it won't stop. I search my pockets for a spliff and find half an inch, barely enough to last ten minutes, let alone a whole night. I cannot go back into the street because if I do I will die.

Dawn comes slowly. It's the longest night of my life. At six o'clock I put my coat on and start walking. I walk along Alcester Road into town with my head down and my fists bunched in my pockets. I walk through the city centre, deserted and frightening. Wild pages of newspapers fly up and attack me. Tramps and vagrants put their hands out and mutter curses. I bend my neck and walk on, down roads I don't know but go north. I walk and walk, crying all the time. I want my mom.

I find her in the maternity ward of Dudley Road Hospital, finishing her shift.

'Mandy, love,' she says and holds my hand, takes me wordlessly to a quiet room with a television on low. 'What's happened?'

'I think I'm going mad, Mom.'

She puts her hand on my cheek and rubs it. 'You're freezing, love. You hungry?'

I shake my head. She bundles me into her arms and I sob on her shoulder.

'You're not going mad, love. Honestly, you're not.'

'I think I am.'

'Well, if you are, so am I. We'll be mad together.'

She sits me down on one of the chairs and wipes my face with a corner of her cardigan.

'Can you talk to me about something, Mom? Anything.'

'Well, we had this little baby born about half an hour ago. Chinese. You should have seen his hair. He was over-due, must have spent those two weeks growing a toupee. And his mother was only a girl herself. I think the dad's gone home to get a camera. And then there's a woman in a room on her own because she's having twins and we're expecting a bit of trouble. What else? June's not on tonight because she's got the flu so I'm working with a new nurse. Not keen on her, but it's only for one night. I'm off in an hour. Do you want a cup of coffee?'

On she goes and I try to concentrate on what she's saying so I can be less afraid and when a nurse comes looking for help, Mom sends her away.

'My daughter's not well,' she says and closes the door.

On and on and on she goes, about the babies and the mothers and twelve hours on her feet and what she'll make for dinner and why don't I come home for a rest and have I got money for the bus because she's not sure she's got change and shall we push the boat out and get a taxi or do I feel like walking? On and on and on she goes until I can let go of her hand while she gets her bag and coat.

I lie in all my clothes in my childhood bed under the narrow window by the door. Mom comes in and strokes my forehead, tells me a story about the new family who have moved in next door and the massive renovations that they're doing to the house. She tells me about Marg across the road and the new car Ken's bought her. She talks until my legs stop moving and I fall asleep.

When I come down in the morning, Dad is making corn porridge. Whatever Mom has said to him prevents any questions.

'Hungry?' he says and I shake my head and sit at the table.

'Course you is. When last you eat? You meagre like when you was a child. Eat this.'

The plate's in front of me, hot and fragrant. He puts a spoon on the table and sits opposite me. If he's nice, I might cry.

'You want evaporated milk? Cool it down?'

I hold the spoon but can do nothing with it.

'What?' he says.

'I don't feel well,' I say. 'I think I'm going to die.'

He kisses his teeth. 'You think you is the only one?' But I hear something in his voice, some piece of worry, some piece of love, and the tears spill.

'Wait,' he says and takes the plate. He brings it back with

evaporated milk swirled into the porridge. 'That will cool it down. Eat it.'

I dip the spoon in, take half a mouthful, swallow it down. He watches.

'Good,' he says.

34

I'm a Nurse, I'm a Thief, I'm a Soldier

'And why do you want the job as Committals Clerk with the Office of the Chief Crown Prosecutor, Miss O'Loughlin?'

I'm wearing a new dress and Mom has given me one of her Jehovah's Witness coats to wear. I've got a handbag for the first time in years and inside are my certificates, O levels, one A level, Shorthand, Typing, Office Practice, Commerce, Accounts and Commercial German.

'I think it would be really interesting,' I say because this is the fifth interview this week and the truth is that I'm desperate and I'll do anything to fill my days and weary me enough at night to let me sleep.

The woman reads my certificates again and passes me a pad and a pencil for a shorthand test. She picks up a piece of paper and starts reading.

'Regina vs Benjamin Southall. On the second day of June in the City of Birmingham . . .'

It's easy but, better than that, it's interesting. It's not Bills of Lading for Tanzania like the first interview or proposed changes to the cleaning contract for the bus company, it's a burglary and assaulting a police officer. I type it up eagerly and give it back to her in a few moments. When she raises her eyebrows, I know I've got the job.

My days are full of dictation by prosecution solicitors, who did what to whom and why and what's the evidence and what's the strategy and which witnesses are needed for the court case in what order and what's missing and how to get it. I type it all up and give it back and start all over again. The days are full but, without a spliff, without a drink, the nights are everlasting.

I sit at home with Dad watching the telly, I go up to bed and watch the lights on the ceiling and wait for my legs to stop moving and my thoughts to settle. Sometimes I'm still awake as the sky turns from black to grey and can only sleep as it's getting light, and I feel safe again. I get up for work, drink a cup of tea and take the bus into town.

One day, I'm taking dictation from Mr Amway, senior prosecutor. His office is on the ninth floor, tall windows, a mahogany desk, pencils lined up by the blotter. He has a soft, sonorous voice, slight touch of West Country.

'. . . under the Offences Against the Person Act 1861 this offence can only be made out if . . .'

I yawn. He notices.

'Late night?' he says. There's a twinkle in his eye. A stout man in a stripy shirt with a white collar and spectacles, an ex-marine with a wife and four children living quietly in Solihull, I know he thinks I'm out at parties and clubs with a boyfriend, dancing the night away, one too many, up at all hours.

'Couldn't sleep,' I say. 'Sorry.'

He resumes. '. . . and this offence can only be made out if we can prove intention or recklessness. Bodily harm in its ordinary meaning must include . . .'

I yawn again. He notices again.

'Worry or excitement?' he asks.

'Sorry?'

'Not sleeping. Worry or excitement?'

'Worry.'

'Ah. I see,' he says. 'Worry and Clive Amway are intimately acquainted.'

He gets up and stands by the big windows that overlook the city centre. 'Lots to worry about in this place, and in this job there is no shortage of subjects.'

He turns round and looks at me. 'What you need is a good book. That's what I do. Have a couple by the bed for the "four-o'clock-in-the-mornings" as I call them. You know, swirling thoughts. A person could start to dwell. No good dwelling. Pick up a book and you'll forget all about your troubles.'

The four-o'clock-in-the-mornings have lasted for months and I am desperate.

'What would you suggest?' I say. 'Give me your top ten books.'

'Oh,' he says, surprised. 'Well, let me see. Pretty difficult to narrow it down like that. Let me have a go.'

He sits back down on his leather chair and taps his fountain pen against his teeth. He screws up his eyes and says nothing for a few minutes. Then he points at my notepad.

'Take this down.'

Fair Stood the Wind for France by H. E. Bates

Three Men in a Boat by Jerome K. Jerome

The Siege of Krishnapur by J. G. Farrell

The Riddle of the Sands by Erskine Childers

Madame Bovary by Gustave Flaubert

Thérèse Raquin by Émile Zola
Les Misérables by Victor Hugo
The Red Badge of Courage by Stephen Crane
Le Grand Meaulnes by Alain-Fournier
The Red and the Black by Stendhal

'That should keep you going,' he says. 'Now, where was I?'

After work, I hurry into the biggest bookshop I know. I find Mr Amway's selection, all of them, in the same place, the Classics Section. I pick them out and take them to the till. I have some money now that I'm not buying weed and hardly leave the house. I put them in a little pile next to the bed, one on top of the other. I have never heard of a single author of a single title so I start at the top with *Le Grand Meaulnes*. It's a story about a boy in France. I fall asleep to the sound of his clogs on the cobbles of Sologne. The next night he keeps me company through crumbling rooms in a deserted chateau, through the quietest dark hours and into early morning. Within a few days, H. E. Bates takes his place, then Childers, Stendhal and Victor Hugo.

Émile Zola describes near-madness in *Thérèse Raquin*, 'falling into a dark, cold hole', and I can hardly turn the page for wondering what will happen to the two murderers, but between the tension and the grief, he tells me that I'm not alone. Gustave Flaubert makes me cry for Emma Bovary, the ordinary woman looking for that one thing more, her boredom, her discontent, not fitting in the right place and then her only way out. I read the same passage again and again.

You forget everything. The hours slip by. You travel in your chair through centuries you seem to see before you, your thoughts are caught up in the story, dallying with the details or following the course of the plot, you enter into characters, so that it seems as if it were your own heart beating beneath their costumes.

They last only a few weeks, those ten books. Soon, I'm back in the bookshop to look for what else those authors wrote or to look for other books with the same sort of cover, the same type, the black spine of the Penguin Classic. I pay for another ten paperbacks in the same vein: *The Scarlet Letter, Main Street, Sentimental Education* – I'm going by title and cover – *The Old Wives' Tale, Of Human Bondage, A Woman of the Pharisees, North and South.* I go by the picture on the front with no idea what's inside: *Daniel Deronda, Pride and Prejudice, The Awakening.*

I sleep easier with a big pile of books on the floor. I go on and on like this, week after week, month after month. If I wake, I turn on the light and reach down. I'm in Nepal, I'm in Brighton, I'm in Vienna. I'm a nurse, I'm a thief, I'm a soldier.

I start to think I might not die. I might find a way to live through books and other people's lives. I might have children. I might grow up. I think of all the books in the bookshop in town, thousands of them, millions. I think how long it would take to read everything, all the Dickens, all the Brontës, all of Graham Greene, Edith Wharton and Jean Rhys, all of Mark Twain, Somerset Maugham and Thomas Hardy, *Remembrance of Things Past, A Dance to the Music of Time, War and Peace.* It would be years before I got through them all and there's new ones every week. I'd be an old lady before I got to the end.

I turn the page and keep reading. I'm going to live.

Acknowledgements

This is the easy part. This is the bit where I make a long list of the many, many people who have brought this book to life.

First I must thank Mary-Anne Harrington who has kept faith with me since she read my first novel and who, through judicious questioning and probing, helped me make a narrative out of a thousand disparate scenes from my life. To everyone at Tinder Press who has worked so hard to take a scruffy manuscript and make it into a beautiful book, thank you.

Jo Unwin, my agent, thank you for your continuing support, a constant guide, reliable and true. Cathy Rentzenbrink, there at the end of the phone, as always, thank you for your wisdom.

I finished this book while I was Writer in Residence at the University in Limerick and I would like to thank Professor Joseph O'Connor and the Creative Writing Department for their welcome and professional support.

To the friends of my heart, you know who you are, my deepest gratitude for your love, companionship, laughter,

Acknowledgements

hospitality and for being there during the pain and horrors of our time.

My brothers and sisters, Conrad, Kim, Tracey, Dean and Karen, all of you are here on these pages and I thank you for your generosity in allowing me to tell this story, for your memories, straight steer and invaluable contributions. We survived, didn't we?

As always, as always, this is for my children Bethany and Luke, the lights of my life.